Praise for Dinty W. Moore's *Between Panic and Desire*

"*Between Panic and Desire* is more autopsy than memoir—a strange new hybrid. It's a fantasy of letting go of the things that have haunted Moore his entire life. These things do, in fact, float off the pages."
—*Los Angeles Times*

"[A] quirky, entertaining joyride."
—*Publishers Weekly*

"Moore forges a brisk, incisive, funny, sometimes silly, yet stealthily affecting memoir in essays and skits, a 'generational autobiography,' and good candid guy stuff. . . . Each anecdote, piece of pop-culture trivia, and frankly confessed panic and desire yields a chunk of irony and a sliver of wisdom."
—Donna Seaman, *Booklist*

"*Between Panic and Desire* turns the memoir genre on its head as it deftly moves from essay to essay."
—Peter Grandbois, *Review of Contemporary Fiction*

"The writing is frequently very funny, insightful, too, especially Moore's belief that humans are generally delusional when it comes to their expectations vs. what is realistically possible. . . . The narrative has its poignant moments, particularly in Moore's recollections of his father. And despite his fractured take on the world, his message is essentially hopeful. Moore, it seems, is moving on."
—Robert Kelly, *Library Journal*

"This book is funny, funny, funny. It is an unconventional—some might say experimental—collection of frolicsome and touching personal essays. . . . The book is a rare example of how unusual form actually helps. It is the ideal display for Dinty's imagination. He daydreams. He fantasizes. He hallucinates. And this is nonfiction. For anyone who thinks the genre is nothing more than a retelling of facts, pick up a copy of *Between Panic and Desire*. . . . It is literary nonfiction with integrity. And it's fun."
—*Oxford Town*

"In intertwined, wildly inventive essays . . . Moore conjures up his, and our, past from a grab-bag of elements. . . . He doesn't work through this crazy salad so much as play with it, using individual motifs as shiny mosaic stones to arrange in funny, intriguing shapes."
—*Athens News*

"From the outset it is clear that our author, a seasoned writer of creative nonfiction, is on a quest of discovery, understanding, and forgiveness. His style of writing is engaging and the structure intriguing in this fast-paced, quirky memoir that is deadly serious."
—Sue Kreke Rumbaugh, *Coal Hill Review*

"This is a refreshing and invigorating book, taking the predictable memoir form in new directions—playfully, sincerely, and intelligently. This is a terrific book."
—Bret Lott, author of *Jewel*

"Dinty W. Moore's prose is crisp and clean, his insights sparkle with biting clarity and magnetic charm. This is an unusual, joyful, and compelling memoir."
—Lee Gutkind, editor of *Creative Nonfiction*

"Hear that? That is the sweet sonic boom of the Baby Boom barrier being broken by this elegant flight of essays launched from the steely hand of Captain Dinty W. Moore in his remarkable memoir *Between Panic and Desire*. Impossible, they said, to reveal this precisely that sense of time, place, and even space. Listen: Read, read, read. Words away! That's it. Exactly. Like that."
—Michael Martone, author of *Michael Martone: Fictions*

To Hell with It

AMERICAN LIVES | SERIES EDITOR: TOBIAS WOLFF

TO HELL
WITH IT

Of Sin and Sex, Chicken Wings,
and Dante's Entirely Ridiculous,
Needlessly Guilt-Inducing *Inferno*

DINTY W. MOORE

UNIVERSITY OF NEBRASKA PRESS | LINCOLN

An earlier (abridged) version of the "The
Little Heretic's New Baltimore Catechism"
was published online at *Electric Literature*,
November 9, 2015, https://electricliterature
.com/inside-information-on-the-existence
-of-god-an-essay-by-dinty-w-moore/.
"The Burning Bush" was published in the
Kenyon Review 42, no. 6 (2020): 69–75.

Library of Congress
Cataloging-in-Publication Data
Names: Moore, Dinty W., 1955– author.
Title: To hell with it: of sin and sex, chicken
wings, and Dante's entirely ridiculous, needlessly
guilt-inducing Inferno / Dinty W. Moore.
Description: Lincoln: University
of Nebraska Press, 2021. | Series:
American lives | Includes index. |
Identifiers: LCCN 2020031220
ISBN 9781496224606 (paperback)
ISBN 9781496225702 (epub)
ISBN 9781496225719 (mobi)
ISBN 9781496225726 (pdf)
Subjects: LCSH: Moore, Dinty W.,
1955—Anecdotes. | Moore, Dinty W.,
1955—Religion. | Dante Alighieri, 1265–1321.
Inferno. | Dante Alighieri, 1265–1321—Influence. |
Authors, American—20th century—Biography.
Classification: LCC PS3563.O612 Z46
2021 | DDC 818/.5409 [B]—dc23
LC record available at
https://lccn.loc.gov/2020031220

Set in Arno by Mikala R. Kolander.
Designed by N. Putens.
Illustrations by Dinty W. Moore.

To Renita, once again, and forever

How can one better magnify the Almighty
than by sniggering with him at his little jokes,
particularly the poorer ones?

—Samuel Beckett

CONTENTS

AUTHOR'S NOTE

Throughout the text that follows, I have capitalized words such as *Hell, Heaven,* and the use of *He* when I am referring to Jesus or God. This would seem to imply some level of belief in the mystical or sacred properties of mere words, but that is not the case.

I went back and forth on the question of capitalization, wasting more time than I wish to admit here, toggling the search and replace function on my word processor. In the end I realized that—like so much of our religious indoctrination—the use of uppercase in these instances was so deeply ingrained that lowercase was ultimately distracting, even to the agnostic eye.

Plus, what if I'm dead wrong about all of this?

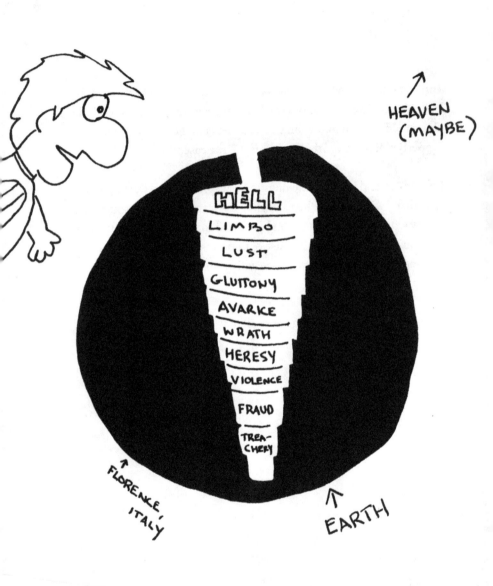

Let's start here:

In one of my earliest childhood memories, my father—a sweet, clever, funny man who drank far too much—is standing in a hole.

A mechanic's pit, to be precise. A six-by-twelve-foot rectangle cut seven or so feet deep into the cement floor of the local Chevrolet dealership's repair shop. This was before hydraulic lifts became standard. This was when a car would be brought into the garage and driven directly over the pit, when a mechanic would need to descend into the hole to access the automobile's undercarriage, to change the oil, wrench off the muffler, or adjust the springs.

My father—his friends called him Buddy—was one of those mechanics, and for as long as I knew him, he dreaded the work.

He hated standing in the hole all day, his blue cotton work shirt spattered with oil, grease, and metal shavings. He hated the fumes, the smells. The constant gashes and cuts on his hands and fingers.

He did what he did to support his family and, frankly, to support his drinking, and he did this for nearly half his life.

Or maybe better that we start a bit farther back:

Say, 3000 BC.

It was about then that ancient Sumerians began to carve odd, wedge-shaped symbols onto clay tablets. Once inscribed, those tablets of wet mud were left to bake under the fierce Mesopotamian sun, and they baked quite hard—so hard that a few of them remain intact to this day.

The wedge-shaped symbols were an alphabet of sorts, and the surviving tablets sent warnings of a dismal, dusty underworld, a dire place where the dead drink dirt and eat stones. About as joyless as it gets.

These Sumerian slabs constitute the earliest *written* account of what we now call Hell, the deepest of all holes, and certainly the worst.

Or perhaps we should split the difference and just start here:

Florence, 1308 A.D.

Dante Alighieri somehow got it into his stubborn Italian skull to write a book:

THE MEDIEVAL TRAVELER'S GUIDE TO
HEAVEN, HELL, AND PURGATORY:
WHERE TO EAT, WHERE TO STAY, WHAT TO SEE

Okay, that's not the actual title. But only because publishers didn't have sales and marketing departments back in the fourteenth century.

Instead, Dante titled his book *Commedia*, and while the Sumerians had cleverly scrawled their vision of Hell into ancient mud, Dante's odd poetic undertaking attempted something even more ambitious: carving a gruesomely vivid image of a roiling Hades into the wet clay tablet of our modern Western consciousness.

And it worked, better I'm guessing than the poet ever imagined.

Dante's *Inferno*, a pulsing, perilous mixtape of Greek, Roman, and Christian myths and images, connected directly somehow to an urgent need in the human psyche to make sense of our inexplicable existence, and as a result, countless readers fell for the adventure fantasy, and fell hard, mistaking Dante's imaginative hallucinations for fact, misreading his vividly horrific accounts as the honest reporting of an actual eyewitness—as if the cranky Florentine had flounced into Hell with a notebook and pencil, returning twenty-four hours later, safe, though singed, with a supernatural journalistic scoop.

But he didn't, dear reader.

He made it all up.

That's fine, of course. That's what artists do.

Yet here's the rub: Over the ensuing centuries, countless retellings, innumerable adaptations, tens of thousands of fiery sermons from

Catholic bishops and Baptist preachers, all those *New Yorker* cartoons and stained glass windows and masterpieces of European art by the boatload afforded Dante's fictional apparitions even more attention, more credibility, more a sense of truth through repetition, until all of it—the woeful, tortured souls, the smothering layers of guilt and culpability, the unending misery—became something church-loads of people just came to accept.

Was it all a dream?

Apparently not.

Understand, I'm not speaking here only of the sincerely religious. The fable of our flawed souls, the troubling myth of original sin, the looming possibility of eternal damnation clandestinely infects even those of us who think ourselves immune: atheists, agnostics, secularists, elf worshippers, and yes, those among us somehow too lazy to decide quite *what* we think about God.

The concepts of Hell and sin—whether we actively accept them or not—have been tightly woven into our core cultural tapestry, fashioning our churches and religions—obviously—but also our legal structure, our penal systems, our views on poverty and class, our classic and contemporary literature, and much of our interpretation of history. Wars have been fought over it. Monarchs dethroned.

Dante's vision, based for the most part on sketchy medieval theology, has led to all of that and—in the end—has shaped far too much of what it means to be human, of how we experience our limited and precious time alive and somewhat kicking.

But why?

Or at least, why still?

Mankind long ago let go of the notion that the Earth is flat, that witches pluck eyeballs from innocent newts. We understand why the sky occasionally cracks with earth-shaking thunder and what causes plagues of locusts or frogs.

We no longer believe that little babies are delivered by stork.

Yet we cling fervently to this notion of our inherent sinfulness and the idea that we might suffer mightily at the end, not just for a while, but *forever*.

For *eternity.*

Does this gruesome formulation make our lives more tolerable, more productive, more worth our limited time?

I don't think so.

My poor father, for instance, stuck day after day in that hole—the real one at Dailey's Chevrolet Auto Sales and the shadow one hidden somewhere in his guilt-swollen gut—believed he was inherently bad.

My intellect reassures me regularly that I am probably just fine the way I am—a bit flawed, but a reasonably good person working it through. Yet after years of Catholic school, religious guilt, and persistent cultural conditioning, the feelings of inadequacy are impossible to shake. Like a black snake eating its own tail, I keep coming back around to hating myself for my various "sins" and weaknesses.

Then I catch myself, feel a little better.

But the snake always seems to circle.

The World Health Organization estimates that three hundred million people around the world suffer some sort of depression. That's a lot of people; but imagine if the WHO kept statistics for "occasional self-loathing."

All around me, I see people who walk day after day through their precious lives with a fearful cringe in their demeanor, as if the worst might befall us at any moment.

And if you believe those who claim to know the will of God, it very well might.

Well, dammit, Dante.

You can go to Hell for all I care.

Me?

I'm not planning to.

To Hell with It

1

CANTOS
I – III

CANTOS I–III: DINTY'S INFERNO

Dinty's Inferno

Midway on our life's journey, I found myself
In dark woods, the right road lost. To tell
About those woods is hard—so tangled and rough.
~ Dante, *Inferno*, Canto I

Midway on *my* life's journey, I found myself
In dark woods, the right road lost. To tell
About those woods is hard—so let's just skip ahead.

Late one dismal evening, I blundered toward a distant hill
But soon my way was blocked by three slavering beasts.
Leopards? Tigers? Maybe groundhogs. It was dark.

Then, a figure appeared, stooped and spectral.
The soggy beasts waddled off, pierced with terror.
I cried to this human shape. "Help me, I'm lost."

He turned, and soon I perceived the crooked nose,
The ink-stained hands, the laurel-leafed cap, and I knew:
It was Dante, cartographer of the Inferno.

The Poet lowered his fretful brow, promised me
Ghastly sights of the wretched and the damned,
Images so horrifying I would never sleep again.

"Wonderful," I thought. "As if I'm not depressed enough,
Being midway on my life's journey and all that."
I simply nodded though, cringed, and shuffled forth.

Old Dante grinned, bequeathed me a nickname:
"You are *Piccola Merda*." And I knew then
That we would be great friends.

We climbed a dreary hillside, then down a murky valley.
Soon, a dark portal, topped with a rough wooden sign,
inscribed: "*Lasciate ogne speranza, voi ch'entrate.*"

Knowing not the language, I asked my Florentine friend to explain.
"It's complicated," he muttered. "But loosely translated:
'All of us. Each and every one of us. We're basically screwed.'"

2

CANTO IV

Pudgy, Smiley, Jughead, and Fritz

> Here we encountered
> No laments that we could hear—except for sighs
> That trembled the timeless air: they emanated
>
> From the shadowy sadnesses, not agonies,
> Of multitudes of children and women and men.
> ~ Dante, *Inferno*, Canto IV

Dante's first stop in his marathon poem is Limbo, a liminal location where "multitudes of children and women and men" sigh and tremble, in "shadowy sadness," stuck neither here nor there for all of eternity.

You won't find Limbo anywhere in the Bible. This improbable opening to the poet's nine-circled Hell exists because, back in the day, medieval theologians needed to plug a cavernous hole in the logic of the religion they were eagerly trying to codify, and what they came up with was, to put it bluntly, entirely improbable.

To wit:

Because Adam and Eve liked fruit, they unknowingly ate from the tree of knowledge. This disappointed the Creator greatly. (He hadn't seen it coming, which begs so many other questions.) In his disappointment, God cast them out from Eden, and from a state of innocence.

So they were bad, and like all of us who act badly, they had to live with the consequences of their rash, snake-inspired decision.

Fair enough.

But God wasn't just disappointed in Adam and Eve, He was *really, quite sincerely* disappointed, so He passed that guilt on to Adam and Eve's still unborn sons, Cain and Abel, and then on to their sons and daughters, and then on to everyone who came thereafter, every single subsequent relative of the original bad news couple.

Which, it turns out, means every single human being on the planet.

Dante relied heavily on the work of St. Augustine in shaping his version of Limbo. An ardent early interpreter of Christianity's more esoteric wrinkles, Augustine championed the novel idea that because of original sin, even innocent newborns—if they kicked their tiny little buckets prior to being baptized—would die in an essentially sinful state and thus could not plausibly go to Heaven.

And it wasn't just babies. By the logic of original sin, *anyone* who failed to be baptized could not enter Heaven, even those good people who had had led spotless, exemplary lives.

Augustine, understand, was a great and devout man, a spiritual genius, and honestly, a bit of a wackadoodle.

Here is Augustine in his own words:

> Myself when I was deliberating upon serving the Lord my God now, as I had long purposed, it was I who willed, I who nilled, I, I myself. I neither willed entirely, nor nilled entirely. Therefore was I at strife with myself, and rent asunder by myself. And this rent befell me against my will, and yet indicated, not the presence of another mind, but the punishment of my own. Therefore it was no more I that wrought it, but sin that dwelt in me; the punishment of a sin more freely committed, in that I was a son of Adam.

If you believe in miracles, here's one: it is Augustine's writing that made him famous.

Augustine's prose is certainly perplexing, so let me paraphrase. In essence, he is telling us that he was filled with a nagging angst, and since the source of that angst was not clear to him (see my later chapter on Lust), this dis-ease must have been rooted inside of him since birth, the seed of Adam's sin, embedded in us all.

We are born sinners: little babies, wide-eyed and grasping, lousy with wickedness.

That's Augustine's uplifting message.

All of this is problematic enough to anyone willing to mull it over for fifteen seconds or so, yet Augustine's revelations raised an even bigger problem. Where do we send the bawling infants, if they die before baptism can cleanse their sin? And what about all of those basically well-behaved pagans living in distant but non-Christian lands? Do we send them straight to Hell, just because they lack a proper sacramental rinsing?

Even to a medieval peasant, one who likely witnessed cruelty and injustice every day of his miserable serfdom, the idea of banishing blameless souls and innocent babies to fiery damnation was hard to swallow.

So Limbo was invented, a place not horrible, just tediously neutral.

My first religion teacher, Sister Mary Mark, strove to put a more positive gloss on the concept. "Dear children," she explained, "please understand that Limbo is an entirely comfortable place."

We nodded and smiled.

"It has most of what Heaven has, but it is not *actually* Heaven."

We nodded again, didn't smile quite as much.

"Because those in Limbo miss out on the glorious ecstasy of sitting at the feet of Our Lord."

My six-year-old brain, slow to grasp the true intent of her words, thought, "My goodness, those must be some feet."

But I came to understand, gradually, what she meant.

The innocent but unbaptized babies and adults would spend eternity stuck in this odd waiting room, experiencing a constant awareness that they were missing out on something.

They were *not* in Heaven. They were *not* among the chosen.

Perhaps the best analogy would be those discontented folks sitting way in the back of a crowded Boeing A380 Airbus, jammed next to the tiny restroom, watching jealously as those in first class celebrate with warm face towels and free cocktails, forever and ever.

And ever.

Amen.

Sister Mary Mark didn't care much about the intricacies of medieval theology. But she was obsessed with The Limbo of Infants; all those tiny ones who, for whatever reason, weren't properly baptized, especially those poor little souls in far-off Africa.

"They don't have the advantages that you children have," she would admonish us almost daily. "They don't have churches and schools where they can learn about the one true faith."

So, to help these unfortunates, we, along with every other classroom at St. Andrews, and every other classroom of every other Catholic school spread across our ethnically partitioned Catholic city, and as I later learned, tens of thousands of Catholic schoolchildren all across the United States, collected nickels and dimes to ransom the godless tykes.

A "pagan baby," as they were called, cost five dollars to rescue in the mid-1960s, and each year there was a contest to see which classroom in our school could save the most little pagans. For every five dollars in sacrificed milk money we came up with as a class, we earned a certificate that was pinned to the bulletin board at the front of the room, and also these additional benefits:

1. The knowledge that we had liberated a blameless little one from a diminished eternity, and
2. We got to give the kid a name.

Needless to say, that second benefit appealed to us the most.

I should point out here that my theological misgivings formed at quite an early age. I recall vividly the morning that Sister Mary Mark began introducing us to the concept of sin, and to the important but often cloudy distinction between venial sin—bad stuff, and you should feel lousy, but, in the end, no big deal—and mortal sin—a huge deal, and if you die before you go to confession, you sure as Hell had better be wearing fireproof pants.

I remember raising my pale, chubby little arm in the air that day to ask earnestly about the sin of stealing.

"But sister," I implored in what was undoubtedly an annoyingly squeaky voice, "let's say a mother steals a loaf of bread because her three children are hungry. Is *that* a sin?"

"Yes, Dinty, that's definitely a sin." Sister Mary Mark wore heavy black cloth from head to toe and a stiff white bandeau under her veil that squeezed the skin of her forehead, giving her a sort of fleshy pink halo. She was quite impressive.

"But say the kids aren't just hungry, they are *really, really* hungry," I insisted, "and the mom—she has no money at all."

Though I had barely stolen as much as an oatmeal cookie in my life at that point, I was already searching out the loopholes.

"Well, God would probably take that into account," Sister Mary Mark answered patiently, fingering the large beads of her black rosary, "but it is still a sin."

"Let's say they haven't eaten in *three* days," I whined. "They are *absolutely starving*."

"Dinty, please, that's enough. Trust that God knows what He is doing."

I enjoyed arguing the finer points of religion almost as much as I enjoyed making my first-grade classmates snicker. The latter appealed to me primarily because this freckle-faced girl named Cheryl Gerbracht sitting in the desk right behind mine had the best giggle in the world.

So when it came to naming the few pagan babies we managed to rescue with our chipped-in milk money nickels, I went for the goofball answer, suggesting "Periwinkle" and then "Steamboat Willie," trying my best to cover either gender.

The class was driven immediately into a pitched frenzy by this door of stupidity I had pried open, and a gaggle of my fellow first-graders quickly jumped through, shouting alternate names.

"Pudgy."

"Smiley."

"Jughead."

"Fritz."

"Children, please! It has to be a saint's name," the nun admonished us, stomping one of her thick-heeled shoes, waving her black-sleeved arms in what I think was meant to be a sit-down-and-shut-up-right-now gesture. "Children, you must take this all very seriously."

And we did, for about thirty seconds, until someone in the very back whispered, "Pinocchio."

Perhaps we were just foolish children, but maybe, too, we had the wisdom of the innocent. Our daily religion class, the exhausting preparations for our First Holy Communions, the weekly confessions, and nearly every cautionary sermon droned from the pulpit on those interminable Sunday mornings, endeavored to fix firmly in our blossoming brains the disturbing notion that we were very bad inside, sinful, immoral, capable of horrible acts, and that—conveniently—the church, only the church, could save us from ourselves.

But somehow, we knew better.

We didn't *feel* wicked. We felt giddy—with our youth, our expanding knowledge, with the world opening up before us, with the power of language, and yes, with the beauty of a good joke.

Laughing felt good.

Being born as sinners?

Not so much.

It was never properly explained, by the way, exactly how our milk money would be used to save the pagan babies.

One theory we had was that a phantom baptizer would be paid five American dollars to sneak, during the pitch dark of night, into a remote grass hut—understand that our knowledge of Africa at that age was solely informed by black-and-white Tarzan movies—and quickly anoint the unbaptized newborns before anyone woke up.

Or maybe, we thought, the parents themselves would be bribed. "Here's five bucks, Mr. and Mrs. Pagan. Just give me ten minutes alone with the kid. I'll say a few prayers and be on my way."

Or did the money go to the kids themselves?

Secretly, that would have been our hope, though it was an open question in our minds whether Africa even had candy stores.

3

CANTO V

CANTO V: THE BURNING BUSH

WHY'RE YOU PLAYIN' WITH HER?

MOSES! IT'S ME, GOD.

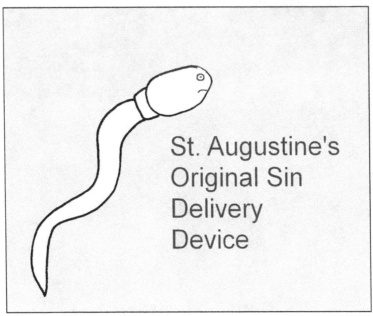

The Burning Bush

I learned
They suffer here who sinned in carnal things—
Their reason mastered by desire, suborned.
~ Dante, *Inferno*, Canto V

Nora Serafini had a toy cash register, made of cheap painted tin. The register was about one-quarter the size of a real one, but it worked, popping numbers up in a small window, ringing a shrill bell each time the money drawer slid open.

Her brothers and I were playing Rock 'Em Sock 'Em Robots just across the living room from Nora. Mark was handling the Blue Bomber while the younger Chris and I alternated turns with the Red Rocker, trying our very best to dislodge our opponent's grotesque, spring-loaded head.

My childhood was steeped in violence and plastic, so the battling robots should have held all of my attention, yet that day I found myself unable to stop glancing over toward Nora, standing there at the coffee table, ringing up brightly colored toy fruit for no one in particular.

~**~

The term "forbidden fruit" refers back to the prohibited apple tree from the Book of Genesis. In actuality, scholars believe the name of the tree, as found in ancient texts, is more closely translated as pomegranate, or quince.

It hardly matters. What was forbidden was never literally the illicit fruit, but instead something meant more metaphorically—sexual awareness, maybe, or quince-shaped parts of the human anatomy.

~**~

If Eve had offered Adam a pomegranate, what would he have said?
No thank you, my dearest. Too weird and sticky.

~**~

Nora was six that summer, and I was just a year or two older.

She had chestnut eyes, thick dark eyebrows, straight brown hair that ended just at the tips of her tiny shoulders. I didn't have a name for the feeling inside that made me want to study Nora's every move instead of playing with her older brothers. All I knew was that I enjoyed watching this girl slide the miniature plastic apples and oranges back and forth on the table. I liked the way she startled every time the cash drawer opened.

My memory is that I did eventually go over and play grocery store with Nora, for maybe a minute, until Mark's sharp rebuke bounced across the room.

"Why're you playin' with her? Let's go ride our bikes."

~**~

At age seven my grasp of the Garden of Eden story was understandably simplistic:

Adam and Eve were naked all of the time, which just seemed silly.

They had a shocking number of pets.

Miraculously, the lions and tigers never ate the rabbits or the chickens. Imagine that!

One day a chatty snake suggested that Eve eat from a tree that God had previously suggested was entirely off-limits. The snake was inordinately persuasive, because Eve—despite the fact that she lived in paradise, according to Sister Mary Mark, and had everything she could ever want—did just as the snake suggested.

Then Adam did so as well.

Shortly thereafter, God popped out from behind a bush and said, "Aha, gotcha!"

And then original sin, Hell, evil, war, shame, guilt, all of the bad stuff.

~**~

For the rest of that summer, Mark, Chris, and I played mostly in nearby Frontier Park, riding our banana-seat Schwinns up and down hills, stopping occasionally to throw sticks into Cascade Creek.

I didn't see Nora around. Maybe she had gone off to camp.

Still, the tiny chestnut-eyed girl dominated my dreams that summer.

Actually, my *dream*, a dream that repeated itself for months and left me disordered and alarmed.

It went like this:

I walk up the Serafini's cement driveway looking for my two friends.

Mark and Chris aren't around, but the garage door is wide open. Inside, the one-car garage is spotless, barren: no rakes, no lawn mower, no bikes, no anything.

Just Nora, raising her dark eyebrows to invite me in, then pointing at a toy casino slot machine resting on a windowsill. The undersized toy slot machine resembles the tin cash register, but with a pull handle instead of keys. She motions for me to pull the lever. When I do, three reels tumble through pictures of cherries, lemons, oranges, watermelons, and finally land on flames, on all three reels, straight across.

Nora laughs, not brightly like the real Nora might laugh, but in deeper register, more sinister, as if she knows something.

In the dream, we walk outside then, into the Serafini's backyard, a yard that extends alongside the garage and behind it as well, ending in a tall hedge. Nora, still not speaking, points downward, and it is then I see that the ground under the hedge is on fire. The flames are low to the ground, but they spread across the length of the hedge, and threaten to come out into the yard.

A woman on the other side of the hedge, the back neighbor, begins hitting at the flames with a heavy garden rake. She calls out repeatedly for help.

Nora just continues to point at the fire, smiling.

~**~

There is at least one other time that God popped out from behind a bush; this one from the biblical book of Exodus.

Moses is said to be hanging out on a hill, tending to a flock of his father-in-law Jethro's sheep, when unexpectedly he sees a bush on fire, a fire that continues to burn without consuming the leaves and branches.

I'll quote the rest:

> So Moses decided, "I must turn aside to look at this remarkable sight. Why does the bush not burn up?"
>
> When the LORD saw that he had turned aside to look, God called out to him from the bush: Moses! Moses!
>
> He answered, "Here I am."

Cleary, the Lord works in mysterious ways.

~**~

My burning bush dream continued into July and August.

I would pop awake, always, at the moment the back neighbor cried for help and began swatting at the flames with her heavy garden rake.

I would pop awake with Nora still pointing and smiling.

I would pop awake feeling shame and fear.

Somehow, I knew that I was responsible for that mysterious fire.

I knew that my reason had been suborned by things carnal, even though I didn't know the words.

~**~

The poet Dante Alighieri had his own early relationship confusion.

The story goes that Dante met his young crush, Beatrice, when she was eight years old, and he was nine, and he fell instantly in love. He fell so much in love that he remained infatuated throughout his life.

For years, historians tell us, Dante would frequent various places in the center of Florence where he thought it likely he might catch a glimpse of Beatrice. He would sit silently, just to watch her pass, which is very romantic.

Or is it maybe just a bit creepy?

It was nine years after their initial meeting that she spoke to him for the first—and only—time. This encounter, the fact that she said "Ciao, Danny-boy," or something along that order, filled him with such joy that he retreated to his room to, they say, "think about her."

That's perhaps a bit creepy too.

~**~

When a few years later Dante learned of Beatrice's death, he began composing poems dedicated to her memory. The collection of these poems became his first book, *La Vita Nuova*.

In the opening sonnet, Dante describes what may very well be *his* first erotic dream:

After the chance meeting, the one where Beatrice speaks to Dante for the first and only time, he returns to his room, he thinks about her, and he falls asleep. In the dream that follows, a male figure appears to the Florentine poet, proclaiming in Latin, "I am your Lord." The figure holds Beatrice in his arms, and she, too, is sleeping.

In one hand, the mysterious figure displays "a thing that was burning in flames," which, it turns out, is Dante's heart, engulfed in fire.

The figure then awakens Beatrice and forces her to eat the red-hot organ.

~**~

What can I say? The Lord works in mysterious ways.

And Dante clearly had issues.

~**~

The story of Adam and Eve has been with us for at least 3,000 years, and probably much longer, given the oral tradition that predates the ancient Hebrew texts. For such a simple story—a few characters and one significant action—it has had enormous staying power.

Not unlike *I Love Lucy*, the '50s sitcom, the one where the goofy, childlike wife is always getting herself into some new kind of trouble and inevitably dragging her patient, forbearing husband into the mess.

I ate the apple.
Oh, oh! What have you done, Lucy? What if the big boss finds out?
I don't know, Ricky. Maybe there'll be eternal suffering? For everyone!
¡Aye Caramba!

~**~

Sex is dirty, wicked, depraved, and immoral.

It will be punished.

That's the subtext of the prohibited pomegranate in the Garden of Eden story.

And we are horrible, ghastly people, because *all* we ever do is think about sex.

All the time.

So just stop thinking about it!

~**~

How did that work out?

~**~

Priests and nuns in the Roman Catholic tradition are required to be celibate. Buddhist monks are too, with a few rare exceptions. Hinduism stresses abstinence. Other faith traditions are a bit less rigid, allowing sexual intercourse—even for clergy—as long as it occurs inside of monogamous marriage.

But except for some scandalous outliers, all religions seem to agree that sexual activity of any kind before marriage is wrong, sinful, to be avoided.

One problem: many of those who find themselves "before marriage" are young, just coming into puberty, or stumbling out the other side of puberty, rather dizzied by swirling hormonal surges.

Picture this:

Two locomotives.

One is labeled "Religion."

The other is labeled "The Human Sex Drive."

Both trains are on the same tracks.

Facing one another.

Hurtling forward at breakneck speed.

~**~

Ouch.

~**~

Which brings us, once again, to St. Augustine, the angst-ridden, willy-nilly bishop of Hippo.

His fifth-century theological writings, most notably *Confessions* and *City of God*, shaped much of the Church's canon law, and thus shaped much of current Christianity. Augustine had his own odd thoughts on sexuality, including some peculiar ideas related to the "disobedience" of the penis.

It was Augustine, by the way, who pinpointed for the first time how original sin passed from Adam to his sons Cain and Abel, and on to Cain and Abel's sons, and so on and so forth, all the way to Anthony Weiner.

Original sin, Augustine surmised, with no biological or theological evidence, passes through a man's semen.

So we aren't, in fact, just *born* sinners. We are sinners from the moment of conception.

Little sinner swimmers.

Evil sperm.

~**~

Augustine, of course, was just as screwed up about carnal desire as our friend Dante.

History informs us that Augustine spent his youth showing his disobedient penis to as many women as possible, and at seventeen took on a mistress—the term was "concubine" back then—fathering an illegitimate son. His unholy actions, which lasted until his religious conversion at age thirty-two, were a great disappointment to his mother, now known as St. Monica.

Augustine's long, convoluted spiritual memoir, his *Confessions*, relates in infinite detail the author's fretful guilt over all of this early bad behavior and his later-in-life efforts to nail down the cause. What he came up with, as you may remember, is that we are all, at our core, wicked, unworthy, and shameful.

And upon that dismal rock, much of Christianity was built.

~**~

Dante portrays the lustful sinners locked in Hell's Second Circle as flocks of birds:

> Foundering in the wind's rough buffetings,
>
> Upward or downward, driven here and there
> With never ease of pain nor hope of rest. . . .

If you've survived puberty, you know the feeling.

~**~

My teen years had me foundering as well, buffeted, driven here and there with never ease of pain. The celibate nuns who literally beat into me the rules of right from wrong somehow convinced me that sex of any sort—even light petting—even *thinking* about light petting—was shameful and perverse, so much so that if I let on just slightly to Mary Kate or Eileen how I felt about them, they would surely slap me, mock me to all their friends, and call Monsignor Flaherty at home just to rat me out.

~**~

I was, clearly and unequivocally, responsible for that mysterious fire.

I was born to sin.

4

CANTO VI

Gobbets of Chicken

My leader, reaching out
To fill both fists with as much as he could gather,

Threw gobbets of earth down each voracious throat.
~ Dante, *Inferno*, Canto VI

The annual World Chicken Festival in London, Kentucky, boasts of "the world's largest skillet," and I'm inclined to believe them: the frying pan in front of me is over ten feet in diameter, forged from hot-rolled steel, and filled with so many slabs of poultry that the cooks make use of garden rakes—yes, garden rakes—to keep the bird chunks tossing and turning in the bubbling oil.

It is *not* an appetizing sight. The liquid has turned to a sickening yellowish brown, and the chicken pieces look as if they are being tortured rather than fried. For blocks around, the air is fogged with the sour smell of peanut oil and burnt hen.

The rake-wielding volunteers manning the skillet come from Souls' Harbor, a "full gospel" church on the outskirts of town. The fact that Souls' Harbor sounds strikingly like a location somewhere in Dante's *Commedia* is not lost on me, but at the moment, I can't find anyone to share the joke.

Everyone is too busy eating.

In a circus-sized tent just to the side of the gargantuan chicken fry, church ladies drop hot slabs of poultry onto paper plates for dozens of gluttonous festival-goers seated at long picnic tables. The demonic horde is white for the most part, skewing toward late middle age, sporting baseball caps and American flag T-shirts, with just a few leather-jacketed bikers scattered along the edges.

I'm over by the king-size skillet waiting until one of the chicken-rakers takes a rest in the shade of a refrigerator truck. Tom looks bushed, his eyes red and watery, but he is polite enough to answer my questions. Over the three days of the festival, Tom tells me, he and his crewmates will run through about 375 pounds of flour, 75 pounds of salt, 30 pounds each of pepper and paprika, and countless boxes of frozen fowl, preparing close to 7,000 chicken dinners.

"That's a lot of chicken," I say, brilliantly.

Tom takes off his baseball cap and wipes sweat from his brow just like they do in the movies. In a hard-edged Kentucky drawl, he says, "Yup, been doing this for more years than I can remember."

"How long after the festival until you'll feel like eating chicken again?" I ask.

He looks toward the bubbling cauldron, squints. "Well, to be honest. I normally don't eat chicken again 'til next year."

Dante reserves his Third Circle of Hell for the gluttonous, and the volunteers manning the record-breaking skillet at the World Chicken Festival seem Hell-bent on insuring a steady stream of fresh recruits.

Myself included. The evening before, I had worked my way through my personal hunk of overcooked, rake-stirred chicken, barely able to swallow some of the desiccated outer edges. Like Tom, I don't at the moment want to see, smell, or taste poultry ever again.

There is, however, one problem:

I am registered as a contestant in the Twenty-Sixth World Chicken Festival's 96.7 FM Kool Gold Hot Wing Eating Contest, slated to begin in about three hours. The festival is held annually in a town that boasts itself as the birthplace of Harlan Sanders, the founder of Kentucky Fried Chicken, and the wing-eating challenge is a festival highlight.

My enthusiasm for exploring all aspects of human sinfulness had led me to register myself some months earlier, despite no prior experience with competitive eating. I have a few misgivings, certainly, but duty is duty.

Morning turns to afternoon, the sun softens the asphalt, and what remains of my good sense softens my resolve. A few friends with experience in eating contests had weeks before suggested that I prepare my stomach with kombucha, a fermented, bacteria-rich digestive stimulant popular in organic food circles. The vendors who've turned out for the World Chicken Festival, however, skew toward non-organic deep-fried Oreos more than they do health food. I can't even locate a simple cup of yogurt for sale, so I settle for a soft serve vanilla ice cream cone, which I know immediately is yet another bad idea.

A spot of shade presents itself near the Sanders Court Stage, and I lap at my dripping cone while watching the festival's "Strut, Cluck, and Crow" competition. Ten contestants—young and old—take turns mimicking a chicken's peculiar lurching walk, flapping their arms, then clucking loudly into a microphone, all followed by two or three ear-splitting cock-a-doodle-dos.

Forty or so onlookers comment on each contestant's poultry prowess, most of the commentary good-natured, some of it downright mean. Remarking on someone's weight seems entirely acceptable, almost requisite, in this crowd, regardless of how many extra pounds the commenters carry themselves.

When a twelve-year-old boy takes his turn, an elderly man behind me mutters, "There's anger in that boy's eyes."

I'm not sure if that's meant to be good or bad.

Eventually, the strutting and clucking subsides, and the announcer, a local disc jockey, informs the gathering crowd that the Hot Wing Eating Contest is just thirty minutes away, reminding all registered participants to check in at the front table.

I hold back, sizing up the competition as the line forms. My opponents are exclusively male, most of them taller than me, or more barrel-gutted, and loosely confident, laughing and poking one another in the stomach. They seem to all have met before, as if they are regular participants in hot wing orgies.

I have two thoughts, simultaneously:

1. I'm not in any discernible way prepared for what is to come, and
2. I've never in my life entered a contest I didn't want to win.

Dante's Third Circle is every bit as bizarre as the rest of his infernal fantasies. As goopy excrement rains from the sky (a literal "shitstorm"), a gruesome three-headed dog, Cerberus, tries to stop Virgil (Dante's poet guide) and Dante from advancing, until Virgil waylays the beast by throwing "gobbets of earth" down each of the dog's three throats.

Amidst this repulsive scene, Dante engages one of the resident overeaters, a fellow named Ciacco, and asks him what will become of the divided city of Florence.

Ciacco offers a prophecy—a future war and the defeat and expulsion of one political party in favor of the other.

This divination, it turns out, is absolutely spot on, perhaps because Dante sets his book in the year 1300 but is actually writing it a decade or so later. Accurate predictions are fairly easy under those conditions.

In any case, Dante (the fictional character) goes on to name a bunch of Florentines that Dante (the author) knew back in the day, and he asks Ciacco where he can find them now.

"Their souls," Ciacco reveals, "are among the blackest in Hell."

When Dante wrote his 14,233-line poem, the label "comedy" basically meant any story with a happy ending.

In *his* comedy, Dante ends up in heaven, reunited with his boyhood crush Beatrice. All of his enemies, on the other hand, end up in Hell, either slinging manure at one another or boiling for perpetuity neck-deep in blistering tar. That's a happy ending, right?

The *Commedia* is brilliant, or so says every college poetry professor on the planet. But to be honest, it is, at the very same time, fully ridiculous.

Dante was a Florentine citizen, but also a municipal official, and as such fully enmeshed in the political intrigue and petty bureaucracy of his time. Florence was not a happy place, and the battling factions, the White Guelphs and the Black Guelphs, battled quite bitterly, primarily over Papal influence. The disputes led eventually to Dante's exile from the town of his birth and a life centered on acute homesick bitterness.

In retaliation for his banishment, Dante populated not just the Third Circle but most of his poetic Hell with people he knew—regular folks, alive and dead, from the years before he was banished—those who had ticked him off in his professional life and those who helped orchestrate his expulsion.

He used their real names. From canto to canto, stanza to stanza, he calls them out and then recounts in precise, excruciating detail the gruesome punishments these rivals suffer, and why their utter torment is so very much deserved.

In other words, the poetic masterpiece is at its most basic level a *revenge fantasy*, in rhymed tercets.

Beyond the macabre dog and the chatty encounter with Ciacco, not much else transpires in Canto VI. The poet, to be clear, doesn't seem all that interested in gluttony. He added his Third Circle, I'm guessing, due to the fact that his hellish architecture was loosely based on the popular listicle known as the Seven Deadly Sins, which more or less originated with the fourth-century monk Evagrius Ponticus,[1] and Dante felt some obligation to follow the pattern.

But in actuality, Ponticus listed not seven, but eight evils:

- Gluttony,
- Fornication,
- Avarice,
- Hubris,

---

1. Evagrius Ponticus was also called Evagrius the Solitary. It is no wonder: he must have been great fun to hang with.

- Envy,
- Wrath,
- Boasting,
- and Dejection.

Oh my! If dejection is a sin, God help us all.

Augustine was depressed about his youthful indiscretions and disobedient penis.

Dante suffered great sadness over lost love and his exile from Florence.

My father, spending his daylight hours confined to a six-by-twelve-foot rectangle cut into the cement floor of the local Chevrolet dealership, was depressed about his father's cruelty toward him, the death of his mother when he was barely four years old, and whatever he witnessed during World War II and never wanted to talk about.

The Sumerians were probably sad about something.

Perhaps they foresaw that someday historians would refer to them as Proto-Euphrateans.

And, yes, I suffer my allotted share of depression as well, both the regular kind and the clinical kind, and yes, my usual solace is to self-medicate with food.

This depressive pattern began when I was ten, just after my parents divorced. My mother had to take on work outside of the home, and occasionally she would stay out with her co-workers into the evenings, requiring on many evenings that I put myself to bed.

Out of guilt, perhaps, she started stocking our kitchen shelves with full bags of Oreos.

I acquired a habit of sitting alone in front of the TV on weeknights, dipping those Oreos into successive glasses of cold milk, surprising myself by so easily emptying an entire package in one sitting.

Trying to fill some hole? No doubt about it.

And I still eat too much, too fast, attacking a plate of food with disturbing alacrity, after which I feel lousy about myself, because my pants don't fit and my willpower is a joke.

Which depresses me.

So I eat some more.

When only about twenty minutes remain before I am expected to ingest more chicken meat, fat, and gristle than any sensible person should ever contemplate, I slide closer to the meekest looking among my fellow contestants, hoping to find some reassurance.

The competitor I've chosen to befriend looks to be in his midtwenties, short, round, and baby-faced, except for an Amish-style beard that rings the underside of his chin. He has the sort of belly that protrudes over the belt buckle before plummeting downward, easily noticeable because his blue T-shirt is way too small. He is as friendly as I ever could have wished, though, and seems equally pleased to have someone to talk with.

"You in this?" Brandon asks me. I've sat down next to him on some folding chairs, and he stares down for the most part, studying his sneakers.

"Yes," I answer. "You?"

"Sure am." He looks up a moment, meets my eyes. "You done this before?"

I avoid the question. "Well, my wife says I eat too fast, that I don't even chew my food sometimes."

Brandon grins. "I'm the same way. I don't eat; I swallow." He smiles and closes his eyes, as if maybe the memory of his eating habits gives him a certain satisfaction.

I suggest then that the two of us should take a walk and work up an appetite.

Brandon glances up from his Nikes again, narrows his eyebrows, realizing at this very moment, no doubt, that I am a rank amateur. None of this, of course, has anything to do with appetite.

"I won this thing the last three times, except for last year," he reveals, making small fists and pumping his pudgy arms for emphasis. "I was sick last year, of course. My dad, he's won it for the past ten or fifteen years, but he's been sick for the past three, so that's the reason I started winning."

I'm talking to hot-wing-eating royalty. He points to his father about six chairs away from us, a man with the same build as Brandon, but aged and balding. Dad's T-shirt is splattered with dark oil stains. I'm guessing he is a mechanic, or maybe just a fellow who likes to tinker with lawnmowers.

"So it's you against your dad, . . ." I say brightly, ". . . against me."

Brandon gives me that narrowed-eyebrow look again.

"I hope the best for everybody," he offers. "That's all."

My new friend doesn't say anything more for about ten seconds, but he doesn't get up to leave either.

"What's the trick?" I finally ask.

This perks him up. Like most people, he's happy to have inside knowledge and seems flattered when asked to share it.

He looks me in the eye. "Just grab you a handful of chicken. Grab you both handfuls, and go for it." He illustrates, with both hands grabbing at the air.

"You hold the chicken in both hands?" I ask.

"No," he laughs. "You rip it apart with both hands. You rip it into pieces small enough you don't have to chew at all."

Like Cerebrus, I'm thinking, flaying and quartering the lost souls in Hell, while gobbets of satisfaction rain down his various throats.

"If you eat the bones," Brandon adds, his eyebrows climbing up his forehead, "you'll pretty much win."

This stops me cold.

I flinch a little, blink, lean back on my chair. I had thought we were eating chicken, not chicken skeletons.

"Yup, a few years ago, I started eatin' the bones." He nods happily.

I don't at this point understand how the bones are going to be the key, though it will make itself clear later.

Slightly horrified, I ask, "So why do you do this?"

"You just get yourself in there and grab some chicken. . . ."

"No," I interrupt, "why? *Why* do you do this?"

Before Brandon can answer my articulate inquiry, one of the 96.7 Kool Gold disc jockeys uses the public address system to begin calling us to the stage, and my name is among the first.

"Din . . . TEE . . . *MOORE*," he crows enthusiastically.

The crowd cheers, probably because the disc jockey's cadence suggests I have just won the Kentucky Derby atop a gigantic enchanted rooster.

Brandon is summoned next, and then his father, and then a second disc jockey joins the first to engage in a few fat jokes at their expense. "Father and son. You can tell just by looking at them that they're champions."

Brandon seems unfazed.

The other contestants are introduced one at a time, and I discover that father-son and brother-brother teams are common. Cameron and then Logan Humfleet are called to the table. "That's the famous Humfleet boys," one of the DJs calls out. "They play every contest we got."

And then Freddie Humfleet.

"That's the daddy."

Then two Dell brothers are introduced.

And a few more folks, until the table is full.

"Also we have here Kenny from the U.S. Army—he's gonna be watchin' over everything and makin' sure we stay on the straight and narrow."

Kenny, our referee, looks a tad uncomfortable, but he's in full uniform, seems to be a good sport, and he rightly gets the biggest cheer.

The long table where we will compete is lined with Kentucky Fried Chicken buckets, and without thinking, I arrange mine so it is centered in front of me.

For this, I am publicly admonished.

"Please do not touch your buckets," the loudspeaker squawks. "Do not touch your water. Do not touch the table. Do not touch anything. Keep your hands down to your side like your mommy taught ya."

Then:

"You got five minutes. Remember, keep your head in the bucket. You gotta stay over that bucket. Anything that drops—bones, fat, whatever comes off that chicken—has got to go in that bucket, or you will be disqualified."

It dawns on me finally what Brandon was talking about: no one is counting how many wings we eat. Instead, the buckets have been filled with chicken, then weighed, and they will be weighed once again when the time is up and the feasting has finished. The difference in weights will indicate how much we've eaten, so chomping down the bones means a lighter final bucket, and—if you don't choke to death—phenomenal wing-eating glory.

"Are we about ready? Ten, nine, eight . . ."

The crowd cheers. I look down into my cardboard pail, into a pile of hot wings that might comprise about seven hefty lunches, and though I've always been partial to fried wings and spicy sauces, and all-you-can-eat smorgasbords, and all manner of free food, I am suddenly not hungry at all. My stomach muscles tighten, my throat constricts, and I feel vaguely dizzy.

"Go!"

But there is work to be done. I grab me some chicken, as Brandon puts it, and I'm reassured to discover that, in fact, it tastes pretty good, which is perhaps also a problem, because I'm not supposed to be tasting, I'm supposed to be swallowing.

I try my best to be ravenous and unstoppable, but four or five wings in and I'm already tiring. I look over at Brandon, his face coated with chicken and grease, and see that he's chewing like a starved dog over a bowl of kibble.

I look across the table at the others and see the same.

"One minute in," a DJ announces.

I shove more chicken into my mouth, but it doesn't want to descend, so I reach for my bottle of water, take a deep gulp. Again, I look around furtively, and no one else is drinking water, or looking around, or doing anything but shoving wings into the pie hole.

Minutes two, three, and four go something like this: I eat chicken, reluctantly, disappointed in myself.

Finally, the DJ shouts "One minute left," and I experience a sudden burst of gustatory endorphins, chomping down more chicken in sixty seconds than I probably did in the previous four minutes, shoving and biting and pulling chicken apart with my hands, seeing that bucket empty out a bit, and hearing an unexpected voice in my head that says, "You're gonna win this thing. You're some kind of animal."

And then the final call, "Hands down, drop everything into your buckets."

Folks come around and snatch up evidence of our rapaciousness, and what had moments ago been a frenzy of gluttonous urgency slows down to a painful crawl. The judges—who are, as best I can tell, the disc jockeys and a few festival organizers—confer to the left of the staging area, staring at the collected buckets.

Perhaps because they know that now, finally, the whole crowd is focused on them, waiting on them, watching them, they appear to stretch the moment out as far as it will reach, auditioning various postures and hand gestures as they stand over the buckets, lifting them up onto a small scale, staring down into the greasy messes inside, grimacing and wrinkling their foreheads as if to suggest they are busy computing the square root of the distance between the moon and Harlan Sanders's grave site in nearby Louisville.

I glance over at Brandon, still red-faced and sweating, though it has been four or five minutes since we stopped. He appears to be on the verge of a premature heart attack, while simultaneously appearing fully downfallen.

A fellow contestant—Mike—appears at my side and begins to chat me up, mentioning it was "damn hard to eat like that," and asking how I fared.

Guessing from his youth, his slender build, his jolly camaraderie that he is a newcomer just like me, I begin offering advice, all of it stolen from Brandon: "The trick is you don't chew, just swallow, or don't even swallow—just push it down the throat with your fingers."

Mike nods and smiles, seems grateful for my pointers.

Then the anticipated proclamation arrives over the public address system: first, second, and third place. And the winner is not Brandon, not his bald and oil-splattered father, not the Humfleet boys, and certainly not me.

It is Mike.

The crowd cheers, and I realize that smiling Mike had me for the fool from the beginning. I'd hate to meet him across a poker table.

The contestants begin to scatter, some clutching buckets of leftovers, some laughing as they recount the gullet-stuffing highlights with friends and family, and some, like Brandon, just wandering off, seeming a bit dazed.

But I'm a college professor in my other life—inquisitive, persistent, nerdy, and annoying—so I saunter over to the judging table, armed with bothersome questions. Though I don't have realistic cause to think I did at all well—not based on what I observed during my too-frequent looking-around breaks—I'm in search of facts, statistics, specifics I can throw around when telling my equally nerdy friends about my adventure.

How badly did I fare?

At first the disc jockey/judge that I buttonhole seems all too happy to show me the large piece of white cardboard on which the scores have been tallied and even happier to point out that I did pretty well, coming in "maybe fourth or fifth or something like that," but when I start pointing to the numbers, asking about calculations and such, and how certain numbers factored into the results, he pulls back the tally sheet, mutters "Well anyway, that's how it went down," and hurries off behind the stage.

Okay, I'm not sure.

Not 100 percent positive.

What I'm saying is that I can't swear to this in a court of law.

Certainly not a court of law anywhere near Laurel County, Kentucky.

But what I believe that I glimpsed briefly just before the tally sheet covered in numbers was whisked away was an indication that the judges were not particularly good at subtraction, especially subtraction involving decimal points. They were disc jockeys, not accountants. Decimal points *are* tricky.

The numbers meant to calculate the weight differences in our buckets pre-gluttony versus post-gluttony didn't seem to add up, to me at least, and the tally sheet itself was a mess, covered with multiple cross outs and retries and hastily circled totals.

And then it was yanked away.

If my instinct here is correct, who knows who really won?

Maybe it *was* one of the Humfleets. They should have been awarded something just for having the coolest last name.

Or maybe it was Brandon, or his dad. I very much wanted it to be one of them.

Or maybe it was me. A chicken bucket miracle.

That's unlikely, of course.

So who won?

Maybe nobody ever really knew.

The excitement over, having survived my first competitive eating competition, with my hatred of all things poultry at a peak, I wander out into the festival proper, an eight-block stretch of downtown London filled with food trucks, carnival games, novelty T-shirt vendors, folks selling low-cost bathtub inserts, and local politicos handing out flag pins for patriotic lapels.

I didn't win the hot-wing-eating contest, but maybe I didn't come in last either. While the gustatory rapaciousness exhibited by my fellow chicken-chomping competitors was unquestionably gross, it was also fun, and I don't at this moment feel particularly sinful. Not enough to condemn me into the jaws of Cerberus, in any case.

What I feel more than anything is numb, inside and out, spiritually and mentally.

I walk about four blocks, wincing as I pass trucks selling corndogs, cotton candy, onion rings, funnel cakes, fried pickles, Dippin' Dots, turkey legs, candied apples, bacon-wrapped hot dogs, fried cheese curds, fried candy bars, caramel corn, blooming onions, churros, waffle fries, cheese fries, and nachos-on-a-stick, until I come upon a table adorned with signs and banners promising to tell me the truth about the Holy Bible.

Centered on the table is a white wooden box.

On the side of the white wooden box, deep-black block letters outlined in bright red instruct me to "SEE WHY JESUS DIED!"

There is a hole carved in the top of the wooden cube, so I can look down into the box for my answer.

Like a fool, I take the bait.

At the bottom of the box is a mirror.

And in that mirror, what do I see?

Well, of course: My own pudgy face.

5

CANTO VII

CANTO VII: SOME PRECIOUS BLOOD A SPECK OF BONE

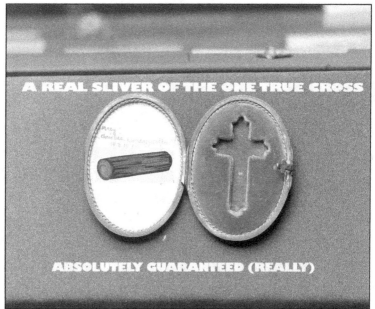

CENSORED

I'M DAMP FROM HEAD TO TOE RIGHT NOW.

Some Precious Blood, a Speck of Bone

> Each pushes a weight against his chest, and howls
> At his opponent each time that they clash:
> "Why do you squander?" and "Why do you hoard?"
> ~ Dante, *Inferno*, Canto VII

A man who calls himself Walter sits on a bit of tree stump, one that has been chain-sawed on both ends and placed on the ground as a stool. He is sturdily built, as if perhaps he has spent the last forty years or so doing solid physical labor.

Tall, with gray hair buzzed close to the scalp, he sits at the very edge of a vast parking lot, adjacent to the Darke County Steam Threshers flea market—a roiling sea of hand tools, kitchenware, hunting gear, sports equipment, dated VHS tapes, and novelty baseball caps.

I've parked my car and am headed on foot toward the Threshers sale. As I pass, Walter calls out to me in a gravelly voice, "How you doin'?"

"I'm doing fine," I answer.

He is sitting in the direct sun, holding an empty plastic water bottle, inexplicably clad in a red wool sweater layered over the bib of his thick dungaree overalls, which themselves are layered over a heavyweight checked-flannel shirt. He wears gray wool socks and weighty work boots. It is peak summer, approaching ninety-two degrees. He is not just sweating: he is dripping like a soaker hose.

I stare a bit, trying to seem as if I'm not, until he speaks again:

"Me," Walter offers, "I'm having the time of my life."

Seems a bit of a stretch for a man sitting on a tree stump, soaked in perspiration, at the edge of a rural flea market, but what do I know about such things?

"Are you buying or selling?" I ask.

"Neither," he grins. "Just having the world's greatest educational experience."

His attitude, if nothing else, is refreshingly positive.

"Aren't you hot?"

He shakes his head: "No, not hot at all."

I make what I imagine to be a vague, noncommittal gesture with my shoulders.

The man grins again, then shares his secret:

"You know," he confides in a mock whisper, "anything that will keep you warm in the winter will keep you cool in the summer."

For a moment, my brain blinks, flickers, turns sideways, and tries to reboot itself in a vain attempt to reconcile the pithiness of his words with my firm suspicion that his idea makes no actual sense. He is dressed for the dead of winter: the wool sweater, overalls, flannel shirt, thick socks would have been the perfect outfit for an afternoon of tobogganing. But he has also rolled the legs of his blue overalls up above his knees, into makeshift shorts, which doesn't quite fit the pattern.

Plus, as I've said, he is drenched. Sodden.

Walter just shrugs, then says again, "Anything that will keep you warm in the winter will keep you cool in the summer."

"Really?" I ask.

"I'm damp from head to toe right now," he offers cheerfully, "and that's keeping me perfectly cool."

The Threshers flea market makes up just a small part of the World's Largest Yard Sale, a four-day event originating in southern Michigan, stretching south along Highway 127 to Chattanooga, Tennessee, then doglegging briefly along the Lookout Mountain Parkway to Gadsden, Alabama, a combined distance of 690 miles. The sale is held annually in August and attracts hundreds of thousands of fervent shoppers every year.

My entry point is Preble County, a rural patch of western Ohio, dotted by small towns, each of them set apart from one another by mile after mile of barns, silos, combines, harvesters, cornstalks, and fields of low green soybean plantings. It is so flat here that if I stepped onto my tippy-toes I could probably see clear across to the Indiana border, twenty-four miles to the west.

Nearly every front yard of every house, every parking lot of nearly every business, every brief patch of gravel or mowed grass between farm field and highway is littered this weekend with old tire rims, used wheelchairs, rusted tools, duplicate kitchen utensils, outgrown toys, chests of drawers, scented candles, chinaware, Mister Coffees, pressure cookers, zinc buckets, loose quilting material, ceramic bunnies, unused greeting cards, iced tea pitchers, comic books, cookbooks, Crock Pots, *Readers Digests*, rickety lawnmowers, and card table after card table layered high with cast-off shoes, shirts, skirts, pants, sweaters, and prom dresses.

Most of the sales spill from front porches out onto the lawn. The more serious sellers—and there are plenty of serious sellers—have canopy tents, clothes racks, and credit card swipers.

A fair number of the narrow country roads leading off the two-lane highway are in sale mode as well, sporting signs, carefully hand-lettered in dark Sharpie against neon pink or green poster board, pointing east or west. The signs are noticeably competitive—big garage sale, huge yard sale, mammoth barn sale, unbelievable ten-family yard sale, super-colossal neighborhood sale—trying to lure bargain shoppers into a small detour.

Preble County, in other words, looks for the moment as if the closet of the world has exploded, and everything inside has scattered out onto the lawn.

Dante knew nothing of the World's Largest Yard Sale, of course. In the Centro of Florence, where the esteemed poet lived until his Guelph enemies rudely tossed him out, virtually no one but the Medici family even had a yard, much less anything extra to sell.

Nonetheless, the Italian scribbler was more than willing to share his own predictably cranky thoughts about our pervasive material cravings. In his chaotic Fourth Circle, poor souls who spent their lives hoarding and poor souls who spent their lives squandering are condemned for eternity to run and collide into one another, clutching the weight of their possessions against their chests.

Which is a fair description of what my fellow shoppers and I experience during this sale weekend, arms full, bumping shoulders and hips as we weave around countless plastic tubs, each of the tubs holding, it seems, the very same crocheted tea cozies, macramé plant hangers, and outmoded PlayStation consoles.

Highway 127 is similarly perilous: at spots, in between the small towns dotting the route like rosary beads, the speed limit reaches sixty, but during the long weekend shopping spree, bargain hunters often slow unpredictably, sometimes lurching to a full stop mid-highway, straining to see across the road, to size up the wares, calculating in a split second whether it is best to pull over or to roll on.

It is a miracle we are not all killed.

The line between sin and simple human weakness, in the writings of Dante and Augustine, and thus in the Catholic Church, and therefore in much of Christian doctrine and theology, is amazingly flimsy and firmly lodged in the eye of the beholder.

In Dante's Hell, infinite punishment befalls those who desire physical pleasure, those hungering for delicious food and drink, and those wishing to possess beautiful or comforting objects. There is, in my view at least, a huge problem with this scenario: these "transgressions" are universal human urges, held by every one of us, brought to the level of turpitude, it seems, only when modifiers such as "far too much" and "way too many" are attached.

Why do you squander?

Why do you hoard?

I don't know.

Maybe we just can't help ourselves.

You never know. We might just need that Mastodon jawbone someday.

If it is not obvious by now—though I suspect it very well may be—I reject the entire notion of original sin, St. Augustine's willy-nilly brilliance notwithstanding. What we are born with, I fear, is not some hardwired proclivity for evil transmitted from father to son, father to daughter, up and down the ancestral sperm trail, but instead a deep hole.

Let's capitalize it.

The Hole, an empty space inside our psyches, one that proves unfillable for so many of us, yet we try and try, and try some more, leading us down our individual, often ill-advised, spirals.

Sex. Food. Material goods.

Dante's Hell, of course, is a spiral.

What better visual metaphor for addictive behavior of any kind: a poor beleaguered soul standing at the edge of a wide, dark, unending Hole, shoveling, and shoveling, and shoveling, forever, and ever, and ever, and the Hole never fills.

My idea is nothing new, of course. This Hole, this seemingly unfillable chasm, appears time and again through literature, film, and centuries of myth and storytelling.

Moby Dick, for instance. What is the obsessive Ahab actually after? What hollowness is the allegorical whale supposed to alleviate?

Or consider the motivation underpinning countless Arthurian legends of fanatical knights searching high and low for the Holy Grail.

What, a normal-sized chalice isn't enough?

We see these hollow psychic spaces represented in *Don Quixote*, in Goethe's *Faust*, in Gatsby. Even in Al Pacino's *Scarface*.

And come to think of it, what was Dante's quest all about?

He finds himself in a midlife crisis, "the old fear stirring." So he embarks on an elaborate journey in search of something, anything, that will make him feel whole again, something that might lift him from his own "dark woods" of discontent.

Poet, heal thyself.

This idea of the unfillable Hole explains why we find celebrity suicides so unsettling. The Anthony Bourdains, David Foster Wallaces, and Heath Ledgers who take their own lives bear testament to a frightening truth.

While we often tell ourselves:

Boy, if I were that rich, that talented, that good looking, had that many lovers, enjoyed so much adulation, owned a mansion with thirty-two bedrooms, a yacht in the Mediterranean—whatever—I'd be so blissful, I'd never complain.

The reality, one we don't want to acknowledge, is that the Hole really is *that* big. Unbelievably big.

Impossibly big, for some people.

So, when the rich and famous take their own lives, we are forced to confront this disturbing, unpalatable fact: there is nothing you can purchase, possess, or achieve that will make that empty feeling go away.

The *Los Angeles Times* recently quoted a study estimating that the average U.S. household contains three hundred thousand objects. Three hundred thousand objects!

We began as hunter-gatherers, and we'll be damned—literally, if Dante is to be believed—before we stop.

That sturdy fellow Walter, sitting contentedly on a tree stump, "having the world's greatest educational experience," was hoarding clothes, I suppose. "Anything that will keep you warm in the winter will keep you cool in the summer," he repeated, wrapped in layers of wool and denim on a summer afternoon when most of us dreamt of shedding whatever we could to beat the soggy heat.

Or perhaps he was just gathering people's odd reactions.

I'm tempted to suggest he was a divine messenger, but his divine message made little to no sense. Maybe it was performance art, though Darke County is not known for harboring avant-garde theater.

Maybe he was a bit off his rocker. Or maybe he knew exactly what he was doing—trying to shed weight, perhaps—and was having a bit of a tease with the nosy, overfed fellow in the round glasses.

That would be me.

All I can say with any authority is that he was gone when I finally gave up on the Steam Threshers flea market and headed, sweat-soaked, but in no way cool, back to my car.

I roll north along Highway 127, seeing all of the same sites: yard sales, porch sales, barn sales, church sales, bargain-dazed pedestrians taking their lives into their own hands wandering distractedly across the road.

A roadside sign reminds motorists that Annie Oakley, the "Little Miss Sureshot" who once demonstrated her astonishing marksmanship skills as part of Buffalo Bill's Wild West show, is Darke County's favorite daughter, born, raised, and buried.

And then another sign, this time for the Shrine of the Holy Relics. Well, I think to myself, can't miss that.

Dante, describing his Fourth Circle, is quick to mention that many of those whirling about with stones on their chests, slamming into one another and shouting accusatory questions, had been "clerics, cardinals, popes" in their earthly lives, and after a short drive and quick detour, I arrive at the Shrine of the Holy Relics in Maria Stein, Ohio, all the proof anyone would ever need that the Catholic Church has its own hoarding problem.

The Shrine (in actuality, a small chapel) holds, I learn soon enough, the second largest collection of sacred relics in the United States. Attached to a former convent for the gruesomely named Sisters of the Precious Blood, the Shrine contains eleven hundred separate relics— bits of rock, bits of wood, bits of cloth.

That's what they look like to me, anyway—chips and rags and slivers—but tiny tags pinned inside the glass display cases indicate that I'm looking at salvaged wood from the cross on which Jesus died (the "True Cross"), as well as a two-thousand-year-old nail used to hold Jesus onto that cross, a "particle" from the manger in which Jesus rested as an infant, a bit of wood from the Last Supper table, and a thorn from the Crown of Thorns, alongside countless bone shards and fragments of clothing from countless saints, many of them put to death for their beliefs.

An amazing collection, indeed, and all the more amazing if one were to believe these relics to be what they are claimed to be.

Alongside display case after display case of tiny relics, the Chapel houses a few sacred remnants of considerable size—leg bones and arm bones, for instance, and the entire body of St. Victoria, murdered as a teenaged girl for attending mass in the early days of outlaw Christianity.

She is coated in wax.

Catholic churches throughout the United States and Europe house numerous dead saints in this manner, entombed beneath altars, some waxy like Victoria, others preserved under coats of silver, or even marble. In some cases, the dead bodies have been deemed "incorruptible," meaning they did not immediately evidence the normal decay expected of a human corpse.

When St. Agnes of Montepulciano, for instance, died in 1317, not only did her body remain incorrupt but it is said that a perfumed liquid flowed from her hands and feet.

Relics are bizarre at best, and at times a bit ghoulish.

Other notable relics scattered about the Catholic universe include the shriveled tongue of St. Anthony of Padua, hair clippings and fingernails from St. Clare of Assisi, the salt-cured heart of sickly St. Camillus, and, until it was stolen a few decades back, the circumcised foreskin of Jesus, supposedly gifted to Pope Leo III by the Emperor Charlemagne.

Any relic said to be directly tied to Jesus is highly revered among true believers, and for a time, I kid you not, eighteen separate European churches claimed to have bits of the holiest foreskin. Most of the desiccated specimens were lost or destroyed over the centuries, until a small church in Calcata, Italy, had claim to the only remaining bit, said to be "the color and size of a red chickpea," and paraded in a jeweled case through the city streets on the Feast of the Circumcision of Our Lord.

Then, in the 1980s, it was gone, suddenly announced as having been "stolen," though many believe that Vatican officials spirited the relic away, embarrassed by the immense unseemliness of it all.

I'm not sure what became of the parade.

Inevitably, I suppose, the Shrine of the Holy Relics volunteers were having their own yard sale, in the convent's "Pilgrim Gift Shop."

Out of sheer habit, I stopped in.

Had I been in search of crucifixes, holy water flasks, mini statues of the saints, or rosaries, the bargains were pretty good.

But I wasn't.

I might have been persuaded to pick up a few wrist bones, foreskins, or nail clippings, as a souvenir.

But none were on offer.

In this way I was saved, from Dante's Fourth Circle.

6

CANTO VIII

CANTO VIII: INTO THE PICKLING SWILL

HOMOSEXUAL STEAMROLLER

WARNING

Fornicators, Drunkards, Sodomites
Homosexuals, Gangster Rappers
Immodest Women
Immoral Movie Watchers
Darwinists,
Feminists, Atheists,
Abortionists, Socialist
Pot Smokers
Dirty Dancers, Gamblers

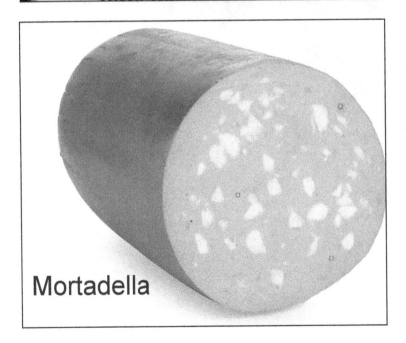

Mortadella

Into the Pickling Swill

And I said, "Master, truly I should like
To see that spirit pickled in this swill,

Before we've made our way across the lake."
~ Dante, *Inferno*, Canto VIII

In medieval Bologna, the bodies of executed criminals, suicides, the excommunicated, and other undesirables were thrown into a ravine just beyond the city limits. Minor criminals were whipped along the edges of the ravine by the public executioner.

There was a saying in Bologna back then, a way for children to taunt one another: "Your father was thrown into the *Salse.*"

Salse was the name of the ravine. It is also Italian for "sauce" or "pickle."

In Canto VIII of Dante's *Commedia*, we find the fictional Dante and his spirit guide, Virgil, crossing a fetid marsh in a rickety little boat, holding on for dear life and arguing with Phlegyas the boatman about how long they might stay on the other side.

Halfway across, a poor soul pops up out of the swampy water and taunts Dante. "Who are you," he asks, gripping at the side of the boat with both hands, "to come here before your time?"

Virgil pushes the fellow back into the foul water almost immediately, and Dante, much relieved, remarks that he would truly love to see "that spirit pickled in this swill."

Later in the poem, Dante asks the Florentine politician Venedico Caccianemico, *"Ma chi ti mena a si pungenti salse?"*

The line is often translated as "What brought you into this pickle?"

Dante is likely referencing the Bolognese ravine of criminals, as well as punning on the word *salse*, in both of these pickle/sauce references. Plus, rather predictably, Dante is out for revenge.

The fellow in the water heckling our fictional Dante, the sinner condemned for all time to live in stinking filth, is revealed a few lines later to be Filippo Argenti, a contemporary of the *real* Dante years earlier in Florence, and likely an enemy.

One historical account has him slapping Dante in the face on a public street; another suggests that Argenti, or perhaps his brother, took possession of Dante's confiscated property after the poet's exile.

In the poem, Argenti is absolutely furious with Dante, and Dante is absolutely furious with Argenti.

Phlegyas the boatman is also furious, with both Virgil and Dante, and they with him.

Once Filippo Argenti drifts away from the skiff, he is attacked by other souls living in the foul mud. Filled with rage, they tear him to pieces.

Everyone in Canto VIII of Dante's *Inferno*, in other words, is mad as hell.

It is the obligation of Westboro Baptist Church to put the cup of God's fury to America's lips, and cause America to drink it. And you will drink it!
        ~ Fred Phelps, founder of the Westboro Baptist Church

Imagine, if you can, how angry Dante—the real Dante, not the character he invented for his *Commedia*—must have been to devote thirteen years of his life writing a 14,233-line poem, in intricate *terza rima*, hoping that his poetic masterpiece might serve along the way to destroy the reputations of those who had screwed with him in his late twenties and early thirties.

That, my friends, is a lot of anger.

A popular photo circulating on social media over the past few years depicts a male protestor wearing a placard, so large it hangs from his shoulders and covers the bulk of his torso. In the photo, you can see the man's red shirt and harlequin-patterned tie, but not his face.

His sign—in large black, blue, and red type—reads:

Whores, whoremongers, adulterers, adulteresses, porn-loving masturbators, sodomites, lesbians, girly men, manly women, immodest and rebellious women, alcohol drinkers, pot-smokers, drug-heads, tattoo getters, party animals, dirty dancers, potty-mouths, blasphemers, liars, gossips, thieves, gangster rappers, rock n' rollers, entertainment and sports worshippers, jewelry worshippers, parent haters, bitter people, merciless devils, occult witches and sorcerers, money-hungry career pursuers, envious and thankless idolaters, prideful scoffers, God mockers, Bible-skeptics, atheists, evolutionists, pro-choicers, two-faced church members, backsliders, Muslims, Buddhists, Hindus, Hare Krishna's, New-Age Guru's, Jehovah's Witness', Mormons, Christ rejecting Jews, Mary-worshipping Catholics, sin-friendly heresy teachers . . .

AND EVERY OTHER FORM OF LIFE THAT IS
CONTRARY TO THE HOLY LAWS OF GOD

**HELL AWAITS YOU IF YOU DO NOT ABANDON
YOUR SIN AND RUN TO CHRIST FOR MERCY!!!**

The man wearing the sign is also, maybe, a little angry.

The question has been asked before: Why are so many fundamentalist Evangelical Christians—like the fellow holding that sign or the megaphone-wielding, bible-waving Brother Jed who every few months visits my small Ohio college town to denounce "whorish" sorority girls, or those deplorable folks at the Westboro Baptist Church who insist "God Hates Fags"—so pissed off so much of the time.

So absolutely livid.

Why?

I'd think they would be fairly happy.

Christians have, after all, owned Western culture for close to two thousand years.

Anger is a sin.

If you don't believe me, ask Filippo Argenti.

Though can you? Last we see of him, poor Filippo is being torn apart by his fellow mud people, biting at his own body to assist in the violent dismemberment.

Can you be murdered while in Hell?

Anger is a sin, yet there are undeniably nowadays scores of very angry Christians. Add this to the file of "what makes no sense."

> And those of you who blame God are very, very wicked, and naughty, and you're going to GO . . . TO . . . HELL! You'll be in Hell with all of these atheists, and skeptics, and homos, and Muslims, and Hindus, and Buddha!
> ~ Brother Jed Smock

Anger is hard to keep under control. Like erotic thoughts, or craving sweet and savory, or wanting cool new stuff to put on our living room shelves.

Dante's own anger is in fact the most problematic feature of the entire Inferno.

~ Martha Cooley

Cooley, a novelist and translator of Italian literature, is most bothered by a scene in Canto XXXII, after Dante and Virgil have descended into Cocytus, a frozen riverbed where sinners are embedded in deep ice, with just their heads stuck above, "purple as a dog's lips from the frost."

Dante surveys the scene a moment or two, and then tells us:

> I don't know whether by will or fate or chance—
> Walking among the heads I struck my foot
> Hard in the face of one, with violence
>
> That set him weeping as he shouted out,
> "Why trample me?"

Dante kicks the poor guy in the head, in other words. They exchange some angry epithets, and then Dante leans down to pull out clumps of the man's hair.

Dante had issues.

Those lousy Guelphs ruined his life.

Alongside our inherent sinfulness, Christian theology promotes the notion that we are meant to suffer during our time here on earth. Suffering is a pretty good way, in fact, of cleansing one's soul of sin and getting a ticket to heaven.

But we don't want to suffer. So it sure is helpful to have someone to blame.

It must, dammit, it must be *their* fault!

Which makes us very, very angry.

Here's how it all plays out:

- we feel somewhere between a low-grade and a highly developed sense of desolation,
- probably because we are bad people, given original sin and all that,
- and also because our great-great-(times-a-billion-zillion-) grandparents, Adam and Eve, were such terrible ingrates,
- and then someone came along and killed Jesus,
- so getting into Heaven is now so damn complicated,
- almost impossible,
- because, in case you hadn't noticed, it's not particularly easy to resist temptation for eighty years,
- and by the way, who is responsible for all of this?
- oh yes, those folks over there,
- the really bad ones, who make all of us look bad,
- the ones who are worse than us,
- it is because of them that God is angry and insists we prove ourselves and resist temptation and fight our simplest bodily urges,
- so we hate those really bad people,
- we really hate them,
- hate them, hate them, hate them, hate them,
- especially the gay ones,
- and the women,
- and "the pot-smokers, drug-heads, tattoo getters, party animals, and dirty dancers,"

- and, really, anyone who seems to be having more fun than they probably deserve to be having since—and this is what really pisses us off—we aren't having any fun at all,
- and yes, they can go to Hell for all we care.

If we do not act now, homosexuals will "own" America! If you and I do not speak up now, this homosexual steamroller will literally crush all decent men, women, and children who get in its way . . . and our nation will pay a terrible price!
    ~ Jerry Falwell

A homosexual steamroller?

How did we come to find ourselves in such a pickle?

So much raw anger.

And all of it clearly sinful.

Except not really.

Not when our anger is truly *righteous*.

Jon Bloom, a popular Christian author, explains it this way: *righteous* anger is not a sin, because "Righteous anger is being angry at what makes God angry."

Except maybe God isn't actually angry, Bloom continues:

And "righteous anger" is the right word order. Because God is not fundamentally angry. He is fundamentally righteous. God's anger is a by-product of his righteousness

. . .

God's righteousness is his being perfectly right in all his ways, all of his manifold perfections operating together in perfect proportion, consistency, and harmony. . . . What God says and what God does are good because they are "righteous altogether"—they perfectly represent his comprehensive perfection.

I must confess, Bloom's logic makes my head spin, but bear with it just a bit longer:

"So, what makes God angry is the perversion of his goodness; the turning wrong of what he made *right . . .*" Bloom continues. "God's righteousness demands his anger over such destructive perversion and that he mete out commensurate justice against those who commit such evil.

"So our anger is righteous when we are angered over evil that profanes God's holiness and perverts his goodness."

You can safely assume you've created God in your own image
when it turns out that God hates all the same people you do.
~ Author Anne Lamott, quoting her "priest friend Tom"

We can easily mock Bloom's pretzelled (and convenient) logic, but tortured explanations such as his are what make Brother Jed, Jerry Falwell, and the hate-filled Westboro Baptists possible.

The most blatant error on their part, or so it seems to me, is the assumption that any of us can ever know what makes God angry. We don't know what God is thinking or feeling (assuming God even exists), and therefore the very notion of "righteous anger" is pure bologna.

As in baloney. Not Bologna.

Baloney, the lunch meat, does actually come from Bologna. In Italy, though, it is called Mortadella.

Mortadella and baloney are seasoned with black pepper, nutmeg, all-spice, celery seed, myrtle berries, and coriander. Except for the myrtle berries, this list is fairly close to the spices used to make pickles.

Fundamentalists blaming the evils of the world on homosexuals, adulterers, porn-loving masturbators, sodomites, lesbians, girly men, manly women, alcohol drinkers, pot-smokers, drug-heads, tattoo getters, party animals, climate change activists, and people who question their authority are full of righteous baloney. Pickled, it seems, in the swill of their own anger.

> The fact is, it's all phony baloney. The fluctuation of
> temperature is real, and the temperatures have risen somewhat
> the last few years. . . . This is cyclical and has been since God
> created the earth.
> ~ Jerry Falwell

Because, of course, *he* knows.

7

CANTOS
IX – XI

CANTOS IX–XI: THE LITTLE HERETIC'S NEW BALTIMORE CATECHISM

The Little Heretic's New Baltimore Catechism

Here, arch-heretics lie—and groan
Along with all the converts that they made
~ Dante, *Inferno*, Canto IX

I don't remember any point in my life so far when I was inclined to believe more than a smidgen of what the Catholic Church was attempting to teach me. Even before I entered first grade, during those interminable Sunday mornings when I found myself squirming on the hard wooden pew while Father Flatley mumbled Latin phrases while circling the altar in seemingly inexplicable patterns, the intended lessons just never quite hit their mark.

I don't know the reason. Perhaps I was born with unusually acute skepticism.

Then along came the first day of first grade and my introductory religion class and my first spiritual advisor, Sister Mary Mark. My introduction to pagan babies, purgatory, and forbidden loaves of Wonder Bread transformed my boredom and inattention quickly into incredulity.

"But Sister," I would whine, day after day, "that just makes no sense."

Her answer was to present me with a copy of *The New Saint Joseph Baltimore Catechism*, a pint-sized paperback offering a significant dumbing down of key biblical teachings, written expressly for impressionable young ears.

I don't mean to brag here, but I learned to read early, and the *Catechism* was likely the first book I ever tossed across the room.

The *Baltimore Catechism* offered thirty-eight lessons, structured in a Q&A format, with cartoon illustrations of boys and girls sitting appreciatively at the feet of Jesus and various saints wearing expressions of either ecstasy or deep suffering.

The lessons went like this, more or less:

THE LITTLE HERETIC'S NEW BALTIMORE CATECHISM
LESSON ONE: THE PURPOSE OF MAN'S EXISTENCE

> Q. **Who made us?**
> A. God made us.
> Q. **Who is God?**
> A. Let me say from the start: had I been the author, *The New Saint Joseph Baltimore Catechism* would have begun with something a good bit easier to grasp than "Who is God?"

Know your audience. If you want to reach the kids, maybe better to focus on some of God's more agreeable creations.

Like this, maybe:

> Who made the world? God made the world. And after He made the world, God also made the zebras and cute little ponies!

Kids like zebras and ponies, and most six-year-olds would appreciate a higher power that chose to bring such appealing beings into existence. The question "Who is God?," on the other hand, leads quickly to various unfathomable concepts.

But Sister Mary Mark followed the *Baltimore Catechism* page by page, and thus found herself on the opening day of first grade religion class trapped in an intense struggle to explain this divinely complex metaphysical conundrum to a room of fidgeting six-year-olds.

"God is the supreme being," she recited patiently, "infinitely perfect, who made all things and keeps them in existence."

Never mind that our young vocabularies weren't able to fully parse at least three of those words: *supreme, infinite, existence*? The larger problem was that most of us couldn't breathe, so intimidated were we by the stern, black-robed woman pacing the aisles with her big wooden pointer, laying down the new rules of life:

> "Sit up straight. No gum. No talking. Uncross your legs. If you need to go to the bathroom, wait until recess, and if you can't wait, raise your hand and eventually I will acknowledge you. No talking. Children!"

The fact that she claimed to have inside information on the existence of God did not serve to put us at ease.

Q. What is man?

A. Man, Sister Mary Mark told us, is "a creature composed of body and soul, and made to the image and likeness of God."

"Really?" one of us asked. "So, like, we are like God, then, and so he must kind of be like us right, sort of, yes?"

Before Sister Mary Mark could frame her response, the room exploded with a volley of hopeful questions. Does God have two legs? Why? Can't he just fly everywhere? Does he have a mouth? How many teeth does he have? He's God, right, so he must have thousands of teeth. Golden teeth! Does he have a nose? Does God ever get the sniffles? What does he use for tissues—the clouds?

It might have been me that asked the "sniffle" question.

Sister Mary Mark was not pleased.

Q. Why did God make you?

A. God made you to know Him, to love Him, and to serve Him in this world, and to be happy with Him forever in the next.

Q. How shall we know the things which we are to believe?

A. We shall know the things which we are to believe from the Catholic Church, through which God speaks to us.

Q. **At what age does a child begin to understand the concept of circular reasoning?**

A. Probably at about six years old.

I was, and am, by definition, a heretic, which—if Dante is to be believed—will land me eventually in the Sixth Circle of Hell.

It is circles and circular reasoning all the way down, as far as I can see.

The early codifiers of Christian orthodoxy constructed a set of rules, then promptly announced to everyone, even those who were aligned with religions that had existed thousands upon thousands of years farther back, that we had to accept these new rules, each and every one of them, without question, because if we didn't, we'd end up trapped in a flaming tomb.

The proof?

It's right there, stupid. Right there in the book!

Sure, but how do we know whether to trust the book?

Oh, well, that's easy: God wrote it.

Interestingly, the word heretic comes from a Greek word, *hairetikós,* meaning "ability to choose." I chose early on to question vigorously.

The good news, however, is that, as a heretic, I find myself in fairly good company:

Martin Luther, Joan of Arc, Galileo Galilei, to name a few.

Not to mention a wide swath of contemporary Christians.

Consider this: In 2018 Ligonier Ministries hired LifeWay Research to conduct a State of Theology survey. A representative sampling of three thousand Americans were asked to respond to statements posed within the survey, and a majority of Evangelicals agreed with the statement "Everyone sins a little, but most people are good by nature," as well as the notion that "God accepts the worship of all religions, including Christianity, Judaism, and Islam."

Um, no.

Well to be clear, my contention is and always will be that none of us really knows what God thinks, but the responses on the part of the self-identified Evangelicals run fully contrary to theological teachings and Biblical interpretations.

Don't just take my word for it, of course. Here is what Dr. Stephen Nichols, president of Reformation Bible College, had to say:

"It is the depth of man's sin that led Jesus to die on the cross. How, then, can a majority of evangelicals say most people are good by nature? . . . The evangelical world is in great danger of slipping into irrelevance when it casually forgets the Bible's doctrine."

Or in other words, the responses are, to be blunt, heresy.

LESSON TWO: GOD AND HIS PERFECTIONS

Q. **What is God?**
A. God is a spirit infinitely perfect.
Q. **Had God a beginning?**
A. God had no beginning; He always was and He always will be.
Q. **Where is God?**
A. God is everywhere. God sees us and watches over us. God knows all things, even our most secret thoughts, words, and actions.
Q. **How did that squirming first grade religion class at St. Andrew's Catholic Elementary in Erie, Pennsylvania, react to *this* news?**
A. We were, to say the least, totally freaked.

Try to imagine yourself at that age, away from home all day, maybe for the first time, tucked into an uncomfortable Catholic school uniform, left in the care of a woman wrapped head to toe in thick black cloth, only her pinched face showing below the starched linen wimple, stuck for hours in a desk—which felt more like a punitive passive restraint device than a chair—and you suddenly learn that God has seen *every-thing* you've ever done, heard every lie you've ever told, and yes, has even listened in on your every stinking thought.

"I am six," you would be thinking, "and already I am doomed."

Maybe, maybe not.

Only 37 percent of respondents in the Ligonier Ministries survey strongly agreed that "Hell is a real place where certain people will be punished forever." Another 18 percent agreed, though not "strongly." That leaves just under half (45 percent) of respondents either in dis-agreement with the statement on Hell or just not sure.

Sister Mary Mark would not be pleased.

LESSON TWO: GOD AND HIS PERFECTIONS (CONTINUED)

Q. **If God is everywhere, why do we not see Him?**
A. We do not see God because He is a pure spirit and cannot be seen with bodily eyes.
Q. **Does God see us?**
A. You bet he does.
Q. **Does God know all things?**
A. He knows about last Wednesday, after school, walking home, and what you did.
Q. **Is God just, holy, and merciful?**
A. Well, there's that time God directed two bears to eat forty-two children for insulting the prophet Elisha. Or that time He killed everyone on Earth, including almost all of the animals, by flooding the entire planet. And He smote Herod once "because he gave not God the glory," and Herod was then eaten by worms.

But yes, He is fairly merciful.

Despite Sister Mary Mark's brave efforts, faith in God and organized worship is rapidly eroding.

Gallup polling shows that the number of adults in the United States who belong to a church or other religious institution has plummeted a full 20 percentage points over two decades, hitting a low of 50 percent in 2018. The decline is likely to worsen, given that younger people are less likely nowadays to be churchgoers. Gallup determined, in fact, that a mere 41 percent of those aged eighteen to twenty-nine identified as members of any church.

No one bothered to ask if the respondents believed in the Holy Ghost, and that was probably wise.

LESSON THREE: THE UNITY AND TRINITY OF GOD

Q. **Is there but one God?**
A. Yes; there is but one God.
Q. **Why can there be but one God?**
A. There can be but one God because God, being supreme and infinite, cannot have an equal.
Q. **How many Persons are there in God?**
A. In God there are three Divine Persons, distinct, and equal in all things—the Father, the Son, and the Holy Ghost.
Q. **Can you repeat that? Slowly?**
A. "Yes; there is but one God . . . because God . . . being supreme and infinite . . . cannot have an equal" . . . but, on the other hand . . . there *are* "three Divine Persons" inside of God.

One of them is a Ghost.

Q. **You're not serious?**
A. There were kids in my first grade classroom not yet able to count to three, or at least it seemed so. Perhaps they were just terrified.

We had already been blasted open by the revelation that God eavesdrops on our worst transgressions—stealing oatmeal cookies, spitting in the water fountain, lying to our grandmother about the broken water glass—and now there is a Holy Ghost, and Sister Mary Mark is getting sweat beads just below the starched white band shielding her forehead.

We had come to school, we thought, to get some answers. Our parents, after all, treated us like children, and, well, we were . . . but it had begun to occur to a fair number of us that the world as it had been described just didn't make sense.

For instance, my neighbor's mom was constantly sick with some unnamed condition and often retreated for days at a time to her bedroom. The kid around the corner lived in a wheelchair and couldn't seem to lift his head. Mark Gunnison's dad hit him with a strap. Kelly McNulty's five-year-old sister had died.

The theology we understood for the beginning years of our life—"God loves you"—seemed pretty reassuring up to the point we became capable of independent thought. Now there were problematic questions. Sister Mary Mark, we imagined, was here to clear matters up. But all we got was this riddle:

"What is three things, but only one thing, and part of it is a ghost?"

  Q. **Are You Freaking Kidding Us?**

  A. Sister Mary Mark offered a metaphor. "Look," she said, drawing a three-leaf clover onto the chalkboard, "three different leaves form just one shamrock." We smiled and nodded, until Constance Ploof pointed out that each of the leaves was just a leaf, not a shamrock itself, so the illustration proved nothing. She didn't use those exact words, but we got the idea.

So the nun tried again. Three candles, she mimicked, the wicks brought together side by side, forming one flame.

That made for a better metaphor, but still, God wasn't made of fire, and there were still *three* candles. We desperately wanted a better explanation.

Q. **Can we fully understand how the three Divine Persons are one and the same God?**

A. We cannot fully understand how the three Divine Persons are one and the same God because this is a mystery.

Q. **What is a mystery?**

A. A mystery is a truth which we cannot fully understand.

Q. **And can you repeat that part about how we shall know the things which we are to believe?**

A. "We shall know the things which we are to believe from the Catholic Church, through which God speaks to us."

Q. **Listen, we are just kids, but do you think we are stupid?**

A. Take out your lined paper, boys and girls. We are going to work on our penmanship.

✝

I'm tempted to blame the decline in church attendance and diminishing belief in theological orthodoxy on Augustine and Dante.

Oh, what the Hell:

I'll give in to temptation. Augustine and Dante share generous culpability for the decline in church attendance and diminishing belief in theological orthodoxy. Their ideas are toxic to the soul.

But others helped.

All of those post-Augustine theologian types, for instance, who devoted their lives to obsessively cataloguing sin and castigating sinners, until every human urge was defined as a level-three threat to our eternal souls. Even our simple existence, they told us, was an offense to God, thanks to the wonder of original sin, transmitted, according to Augustine, through our father's semen.

The "sin crew" took what might have made very good sense—DON'T
KILL ONE ANOTHER, FOR CHRIST'S SAKE!—and bent it toward
absurdity, either by plucking obscure passages from clearly specious
books of the Old Testament, or by being "creative," and maybe a bit
perverse.

Here are a few activities that have been labeled sinful over the years:

- Picking up grapes that have fallen in your vineyard.
- "Sowing thy field with mingled seeds." (Not a euphemism for
  sexual indiscretion, by the way, but a literal admonition for
  farmers and gardeners.)
- Failing to stand up when talking to your grandfather.
- Eating any animal that doesn't both chew cud and have a
  divided hoof. Be sure to ask your butcher about this next time
  you order a roast.
- Trimming your beard.
- Being born on a Sunday.[1]

Most of these just seem silly in our modern context, unless you are a rab-
bit, in which case the fourth one on the list probably sounds pretty good.

LESSON FOUR: ON THE ANGELS AND OUR FIRST PARENTS

Q. **Which are the chief creatures of God?**

A. To be honest, we were still holding out hope for zebras and those
   cute ponies. It was time for Sister Mary Mark to lighten up, maybe.
   But what we got instead was "The chief creatures of God are men
   and angels."

---

1. Puritans believed that children were born on the same day of the week as they
   had been conceived. For this reason, at least one Puritan minister, the Reverend
   Israel Loring of Sudbury, Massachusetts, refused to baptize babies born on the
   Sabbath. Loring changed his mind, however, when he awoke one Sunday to
   learn that his wife had given birth to twins.

Q. **What are angels?**

A. Angels are bodiless spirits, created to adore and enjoy God in heaven.

That struck many of us as peculiar, these creatures who did nothing all day but adore and enjoy. Plus, we had been seeing pictures of angels for years, on holy cards, and paintings, and in the printed *Catechism* that Sister Mary Mark had generously provided to each one of us. Angels looked like grown men, except extra-muscular, with long, wavy hair. Sort of like Moses, but younger and more buff. And they had big white wings.

"Bodiless spirits"? The scary woman in black with the enormous rosary seemed to have all the facts topsy-turvy.

Sister Mary Mark, though, did have some good news for us:

"And you all have a guardian angel. He or she is sitting next to you right now."

We shifted in our desks and looked around. A few of us giggled.

"And that guardian angel is looking out for you at every moment, helping you, keeping you out of harm's way."

A brief, collective sigh of relief filled the room, but as had become the custom, within mere moments our wimpled classroom teacher followed with yet more bad news.

Q. **Who were the first man and woman?**

A. The first man and woman were Adam and Eve.

Q. **Did Adam and Eve remain faithful to God?**

A. Adam and Eve did not remain faithful to God but broke His command by eating the forbidden fruit.

Q. **What befell Adam and Eve on account of their sin?**

A. Adam and Eve on account of their sin lost innocence and holiness, and were doomed to misery and death.

Q. **What evil befell us through the disobedience of our first parents?**

A. Original sin, remember? The part where you are born already in deep trouble.

Q. **Was any one ever preserved from original sin?**

A. The Blessed Virgin Mary, through the merit of her Divine Son, was preserved free from the guilt of original sin, and this privilege is called her Immaculate Conception.

Q. **Dinty, why is your hand up?**

A. Immaculate Contraption? Holy moly, Sister Mary Mark, where do we get ourselves one of those.

YOUR VERY OWN CATECHISM QUIZ

Based, more or less, on *The New Saint Joseph Baltimore Catechism*, a significant dumbing down of key biblical teachings written expressly for impressionable young ears.

1. True or False:

   ____ We are stained, unworthy, depraved.

   ____ We lie, we cheat, we steal.

   ____ We covet our neighbor's everything.

   ____ We eat like pigs.

   ____ We only stop fornicating to think about fornication.

2. Who made us this way?

   _____

3. And why, do you suppose, He did that?

   _____

4. Which of these do you indulge in to an unhealthy excess?

   ____ Fried cheese curds

   ____ Blooming onions

   ____ Nachos-on-a-stick

   ____ Self-loathing

5. That Dante fellow?

    ____ Brilliant
    ____ A bit peculiar

6. And Augustine?

    ____ Definitely needed some serious therapy

7. How about this kid?

    ____ Cute
    ____ Confused
    ____ He killed Jesus

8. How were pagan babies saved during the 1960s?

    ____ Catholic schoolchildren donated their milk money.
    ____ Stealthy missionaries snuck into African villages in the
          dead of night.
    ____ Clandestine baptisms occurred.
    ____ All of the above.
    ____ They weren't, but someone in Rome made off with a
          truckload of nickels.

9. What, said to be "the color and size of a red chickpea," was
   once paraded in a jeweled case through the streets of Calcata,
   Italy, on the Feast of the Circumcision of Our Lord?

    ____ A red chickpea
    ____ A shriveled fig
    ____ Please, just never mention this again

✝

GUIDE TO SCORING: You were born a sinner, and that's really all
there is to it. Sorry.

8

CANTOS
XII–XVII

CANTOS XII–XVII: THE HELL HOLE

DEAD AT AGE 33

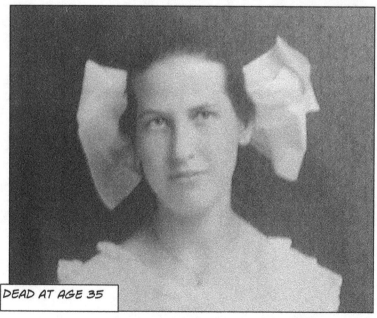

DEAD AT AGE 35

DEAD AT AGE 47

DEAD AT AGE 33

The Hell Hole

Ah me!—what wounds both old and new I saw
Where flames had burned their limbs: the same distress

Pains me again when I recall it now
~ Dante, *Inferno*, Canto XVI

My mother had her favored expressions, and as is so often the case with a parent's words, her voice still rings clear in my mind, decades beyond childhood, more than a dozen years beyond her death.

"They can kick me in the teeth," she would say, during the more difficult moments, "but they'll never make me cry."

Mom never specified who she meant by the pronoun "they," and I never had the courage to ask. And honestly, it seemed obvious enough.

She lost her father when she was in kindergarten. He jumped in front of a New York City subway train, at 157th and Broadway. Whatever was going on in his life that led to this horrific decision is something I will never know, but it was just months after the stock market crash that brought on the Great Depression.

This was twenty-five years before I was born, so my only real sense of the man comes from two fading photographs.

In one, my maternal grandfather stands rather jauntily in a dark suit, wearing a white, rolled-brim Panama hat. The angle of the sun and the brim of the hat darken most of his face, especially the eyes.

In the second, my grandfather is wearing a baseball uniform, posing with a cigarette before, or maybe after, an adult league game, but again, the cap's shadow obscures much of his face.

My grandfather Allan

My grandfather Allan, at baseball

Though my mother lived to the generous age of eighty-four, and though I many times attempted to cajole family stories from the recesses of her memory, she didn't much seem to like remembering. Over the years, she told me nothing about her father except that he worked for the family printing business, and that his parents, her grandparents, eventually retired to Florida.

She visited her paternal grandparents in their retirement once, in her early teens. When she would talk about this visit, even seven decades later, her face would take on a wistful expression, and I could clearly see that the brief visit was a cherished moment in her childhood.

Mom was even more reticent when it came to memories of her mother.

I've seen only one photograph of my grandmother Agnes, who died at age thirty-five, just five years after her husband committed suicide. The picture is a bit out of focus, though my grandmother looks to be in her young twenties, or even younger. Her hair is tied in an enormous white bow.

Mom never discussed the cause of her mother's death, but I have my suspicions.

Agnes and Allan were separated, living in separate states, when he jumped in front of that train. She was alone with two children and dim prospects. It was, as I said before, just after the start of the Great Depression, and perhaps she had great depression as well.

There are, it seems, countless holes in the family story.

On particularly bad days, my mother also used to say this:

"*My* Hell is right here on Earth."

My mom never spoke much theology, by which I mean this: she passed along to me the idea that it was important to go to church on Sundays, because that is what she learned from the priests and nuns when she was in Catholic school, but in all of my memory, I don't think she ever indicated anything more about her religious views, whether

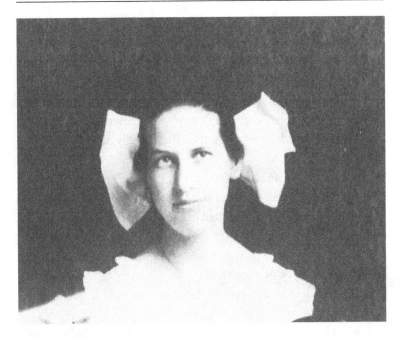

My grandmother Agnes

she did or did not believe in God, whether she did or did not have firm ideas about what might happen after we die.

But she made the glum comment "*My* Hell is right here on Earth" more than a few times, often in response to something that I or one of my older sisters had done to make her unhappy.

There is no denying that my mother lived a sorrow-ridden life: after her mother passed, she was taken in by her mother's older sister, coping somehow with the premature death of both parents during a time when people professed, "It is best not to talk about those things."

She married my father in her early twenties, never expecting, I assume, that she would soon be raising three children of her own, alongside a husband who went straight to the bar every day after work. And before noon on the weekends.

For years, our Friday afternoon ritual was to drive to the Chevy dealer just before my father's shift ended, so either I or my sister could go into the repair shop and convince him to turn over his paycheck, before he spent it all on cards and Canadian whiskey.

So if there is such a thing as Hell, or purgatory, and if there is a God, and if that God allows some people to pay off whatever debt they owe for their sins ahead of time—"Hell on Earth"—my mother would no doubt qualify.

It was unsettling, though, to think that I was part of that Hell.

It was a lot for a ten-year-old boy to reconcile, that look on her face when I misbehaved or disappointed her, the idea that I was a key source of her suffering.

It was a lot to reconcile later in life when I moved away, when she asked "when are you visiting," and I said, "not anytime soon, I'm busy at work," and I'd hear the air go out of her, feel her sinking into her own depressive hole.

It was a lot to reconcile when my own depression welled up, and I thought, what good am I if I can't even please my mother.

There is a third expression I remember Mom using: "It's enough to make your blood boil."

My favorite Florentine poet must have heard that phrase somewhere in his own past, or perhaps he invented it, because in his Seventh Circle of Hell—a crowded one, housing murderers, robbers, plunderers, tyrants, suicides, blasphemers, sodomites, and the profligate—those who have committed violence against a neighbor bob like corks for eternity in a river of blood. Boiling blood, in fact. The sorry sinners are immersed in the fiery fluid, deeper and deeper according to the severity of their wickedness.

Dante's imagination, if nothing else, was vivid.

There are holes in the family story on my father's side as well.

My great-grandfather James Moore was at some point divorced from my great-grandmother Julia. I never determined why, but I do know that when he passed away, Julia arranged for him to be buried many miles away from the Catholic cemetery where she would eventually be interred alongside her son, my grandfather.

It took a concerted effort on my part to actually find my great-grandfather's grave, or rather the burial records, when my curiosity sent me on the hunt. The grave itself was either unmarked or the small stone marker had entirely worn away by the time I located the small cemetery on the outskirts of my hometown. His name was recorded in the cemetery's records, along with the section where he had been buried, and that's about all that I know.

His son, William J. Moore, was my paternal grandfather. Once again, I never met the man because he died seventeen years before I was born. His wife, my father's mother, also an Agnes, passed away even earlier, when my father was only four.

I missed out on having grandparents entirely, as it turned out. They were all four dead long before I poked my head up into the world, and that feels like a hole as well.

Like my mother, Dad tended to change the subject when I asked about his childhood memories. I'm not sure he remembered much about his mom, given his age when she died. His father—a robust, gregarious wheeler-and-dealer type who speculated in real estate, owned a popular downtown tavern, and once ran for mayor, unsuccessfully—faced with the prospect of single-handedly raising and nurturing three children under the age of five, turned over most of the child-rearing responsibility to his sister and his aunt Ninnie.

There are more photos from my dad's side of the family than the few that survived of my mother's parents. For instance, there is one of my grandfather, William, holding a young, swim-suited version of my father and his sister, my aunt Mary, in a swimming pool, on vacation somewhere. He looks proud and happy, though other relatives have described him as mean and openly disappointed that my father, skinny and weakened by severe pollen allergies, wasn't the tough athlete son he would have preferred.

The one photo I have of my father's mother shows her, her husband (my grandfather), my father, and his sister Mary on vacation in Florida, posing in front of a fake backdrop of palm trees.

Everyone looks pretty happy, but photos can lie.

She died the following year.

My dad grew up with his own sizeable abyss, a dark hole in his life shaped by the early loss of his mother and a father's constant criticism. He failed two attempts at college—because his drinking was already a problem—went off to World War II, where God only knows what he witnessed, and ended up a kind, smart, funny adult man with a severe stutter, lifelong alcoholism, a wife and three children he barely knew, and no better job prospect than standing in a rectangular hole cut into the cement floor of the Dailey's Chevrolet dealership and repair shop.

He deserved better.

Both of them did.

"Ah me!–what wounds both old and new I saw / Where flames had burned their limbs: the same distress / Pains me again when I recall it now," Dante wrote, and though I seldom agree with the vengeful old poet-crank, the distress flowing through every branch of my ancestral tree does pain me, still, as I recall it now.

So much tragedy and sadness pouring through one family.

Which begs the question, the one I keep asking here in different ways:

Were my parents and these other people I never knew, my phantom grandparents and great-grandparents, woefully unhappy because they were sinners?

Or were they depressed, in some cases to the point of suicide, because their natural human weaknesses had been *defined* as horrible and sinful? Because they feared that when dead, the crushing agony of Hell might be their fate, forever and ever.

Is that any way to live?

My grandfather William, with my aunt Mary and my father

And how could they not fear death, given the Church's teachings?

A death that none of us can avoid?

Fear of death has its own name: thanatophobia.

In some people, thanatophobia presents as anxiety over the actual moment of dying. We worry perhaps: Will it be painful?

For others, the dread is focused instead on what comes after; and that, when you think it through, is a two-sided blade:

My grandmother, also an Agnes, with my grandfather William, my aunt Mary, and my father

One side slices at those who, like me, are convinced that Hell is a bunch of theological hooey, but still we find ourselves somehow unable to quell that insecure little voice always whispering, "But what if I'm wrong?"

The other edge cuts at true believers, who must tread a highly precarious path and too often live in constant fear of that one small navigational error.

Look at who Dante has thrown into Hell:

Everyone, it seems. The horrible but also the slightly misbehaved. The egregious and the weak-willed.

Consider those he dropped into the Seventh Circle alone: the clearly violent, surely, but also the wasteful. Who hasn't wasted something, sometime?

And don't get me started again on lust and gluttony. It is a bit embarrassing to think how much of my leisure time over the years has been spent fantasizing about either sex or food. (The ratio changes as we age.)

I don't think I'm alone in this.

In his Pulitzer Prize–winning book, *The Denial of Death*, cultural anthropologist Ernest Becker makes the case for how deeply thanatophobia's tendrils reach into the human experience. Becker posits that a fair number of our obsessive fears are, when you get right down to it, substitutes for our primary dread of an unknown end.

Take claustrophobia, for instance—fear of the casket. Fear of that six-foot-deep hole in which we are ultimately trapped for all time.

Or consider those frenetic people—we all know a few—who surround themselves constantly with music, boisterous friends, shouting and cheering, an exhausting, relentless, somewhat frantic celebration. In these cases, Becker suggests, our death anxiety creates an unavoidable need to remind ourselves at every waking moment that, yes, we are still very much alive.

Obsessive-compulsive disorder, hypochondria, and various eating disorders might also connect back to our terminal angst. These conditions center on dictating our environment and controlling what happens to our bodies, perhaps because we know that in the end we lack jurisdiction over the one thing we wish to control: death, and what takes place afterward.

My parents were depressed, for reasons that seem obvious when I look at the circumstances of their childhoods, and perhaps for other reasons that I'll never know or fully understand.

My father turned to drinking.

My mother grew emotional armor as thick and solid as the marble in St. Peter's Basilica.

My own malaise was diagnosed somewhere in my early thirties, but the more I learned about clinical depression, the more it became clear that even my youngest memories, those foggy pre-kindergarten years, were already marked by regular bouts of hopelessness. Even at five, at ten, at fifteen, I was often alone, often in my room, wondering what was wrong with me, why I was so bad.

I was luckier than some. I managed to stumble through college despite our family's dire finances: working menial jobs, and eventually landing a position at a newspaper. I married, and that marriage has lasted thirty-seven years. I still love my wife, and she tolerates me. I've had a career, with the expected bumps, but no freefalls. I have a brilliant daughter.

Yet despite all of this good fortune, some of it providential, much of it hard-earned, every chapter of my life has included dark periods, brooding, crippling insecurity, the inability to be the best version of myself because something powerful and unseen wanted always to pull me downward. I can't not wonder what life would have been like without this depression.

Depression is a hole.

A hole is a place to bury yourself.

And sadly, those of us who find ourselves stuck in these holes tend to dig ourselves in deeper over time, rather than finding a way to lift ourselves out.

In the end, my mother surprised me.

Despite all the good reasons she certainly had to fear her own death, she appeared entirely unconcerned as she rounded the corner toward eighty, faced with the likelihood that life was winding down.

She had little money in the bank, but still for many years I urged her to write out a simple will, one that would cover standard end-of-life issues, such as her wishes for burial. Each time I raised the subject, she would nod, then promise, "Yes, Dinty, of course, *when the time comes.*"

Any easy deflection, I suppose, sidestepping the fact that, under a fair number of conceivable scenarios, she would be dead when the time came and couldn't then clarify anything.

It occurred to me a few years ago that waiting until "the time came" was my mom's own variation on death anxiety. The lack of a will, the absence of any preparation or acknowledgment, meant my mother wasn't ready, and if she wasn't ready, well then she couldn't go.

But of course, life has its own plans.

At the age of eighty-three, Mom was diagnosed with pancreatic cancer—the first significant illness of her life, actually—and was told that she had—best case—six months to live.

It was a shock at first, for her, and for me, and for my sisters, but within days my mother seemed to put any concern right out of her mind.

"How you feeling?" I asked her on the phone just forty-eight hours after the oncologist offered the grave prediction. "Is there anything you want to talk about?"

She acted surprised by my question, as if she had no idea to what I was referring. "Why would I?"

There was a long silence, after which, as best I recall, I stammered something like, "Well, you know . . . you've had some pretty big . . . news . . . just recently . . ."

"Oh, that," she answered. "I'm not even thinking about that."

For three months after the doctor's blunt diagnosis, my mother seemed to truly revel in unexpected visits from nieces and nephews and the steady influx of inspirational cards, potted shamrocks, and cut flowers. She was past eighty, a time in life when a person is often most lonely, often most in need of companionship, so I guess she enjoyed the unanticipated attention.

Her only concern about the coming end of life, or the only concern she was willing to make apparent to those around her, involved nailing down which of her children or grandchildren would end up with which of the many bits of Pyrex dishware she had bought at some yard sale or other. She would hold the various casseroles and baking dishes up, over and over, cajoling me to want it, and if I relented finally and said "Yes, I can use that," she would swoon with relief and gratitude, quickly writing my name on a piece of masking tape and attaching it to the bottom.

Even in her final two months, mostly bedridden and shedding weight at an alarming pace, my mother avoided, outwardly at least, any morbid thoughts or end-of-life regrets. I remember her waking from a fevered sleep one evening, surprising my sister and me in an adjoining room, announcing out of the blue, "Come on now, this will be over and done with soon. Let's get organized."

During her more lucid moments, she actively sought out ways to lighten the mood, insisting, for instance, on calling the nuns who came in and out of her apartment as hospice caretakers Klondikes rather than Benedictines.

Or maybe that was just a side effect of her strong painkiller OxyContin, which she eventually started calling "my oxymoron."

Soon enough we all called it that, even the Klondikes.

For a woman who had endured so much pain, one who insisted they could kick her in the teeth but "they'd never make me cry," a woman who believed at times that her life was but a taste of Hell, the odd lightness of her mood seemed its own oxymoron, an embodied contradiction.

And strangely, she had us laughing too, almost to the end.

One Thursday afternoon, a very elderly, painfully frail Father Carter entered my mother's bedroom, because it seemed the time had come to administer the last rites, something she had requested we arrange a few weeks earlier. My mother was never much for church or priests over the years, but she too must have had her "What if I'm wrong about this?" moments.

At that point, Mom had for days been in and out of an uneasy, comatose sleep, her body shutting down, the hospice workers told us, but she would occasionally revive, open her eyes, and ask for water.

Father Carter was doing his best, but his hands were shaky, his eyesight poor, and at a key moment in the solemn Roman Catholic sacrament, he called my mother, Cathy, by the wrong name. "Karen," I think it was, or something similar.

"Oh," my mother responded quite loudly, startling everyone at her bedside. "Don't worry about that old priest. He's not all there."

Then she turned to my sister Susan, in tears at her side, waved and smiled.

Two days later she was gone.

I don't believe in Heaven.

    I know she's not in Hell.

    I don't know where she is, or where we go.

    There is, perhaps, a hole in my thinking.

I'm most drawn to a version of Heaven and Hell shared by Pema Chödrön, the Tibetan Buddhist nun and teacher, in her book *The Wisdom of No Escape*:

> A big burly samurai comes to the wise man and says, "Tell me the nature of heaven and hell." And the roshi looks him in the face and says: "Why should I tell a scruffy, disgusting, miserable slob like you?" The samurai starts to get purple in the face, his hair starts to stand up, but the roshi won't stop, he keeps saying, "A miserable worm like you, do you think I should tell you anything?" Consumed by rage, the samurai draws his sword, and he's just about to cut off the head of the roshi. Then the roshi says, "That's hell."
>
> The samurai . . . gets it, that he just created his own hell; he was deep in hell. It was black and hot, filled with hatred, self-protection, anger, and resentment, so much so that he was going to kill this man. Tears fill his eyes and he starts to cry and he puts his palms together and the roshi says, "That's heaven."

My grandparents and parents had gaping holes in their life stories, and no doubt painful emotional holes in their lives, as do so many of us. I'm no different.

As I write this, I am one year older than my father was the year he died, and looking back, I see my life so far as one attempt after another to seal the void, plug the crater, erase the absence that defined me. That sounds a bit dramatic, I know, but it is true.

Each year the hole becomes a little smaller.

I hope to live long enough to someday see it filled.

9

CANTOS
XVIII–XXX

CANTOS XVIII–XXX: BRING ON THE ASS TRUMPETS

The boy who
came back
from heaven

*A remarkable account of miracles, angels,
and life beyond this world*

a true story

Bring on the Ass Trumpets

But first
Each signaled their leader with the same grimace:
Baring their teeth, through which the tongue was pressed:

And the leader made a trumpet of his ass.
~ Dante, *Inferno*, Canto XXI

CHAPTER ONE
AT THE CROSSROADS

The leaves barely clung to the old oaks lining the highway that cool November morning. As Alex and I drove to the church in my old Honda Civic, I finally began to relax from the sense of hurry I had felt while getting my oldest son dressed and out the door.[1]

---

1. In 2010 Tyndale House published *The Boy Who Came Back from Heaven: A Remarkable Account of Miracles, Angels, and Life Beyond this World.* The authors were listed as Kevin and Alex Malarkey. At the time, Kevin Malarkey was a Christian therapist living outside of Columbus, Ohio. Alex was Kevin's then twelve-year-old son.

CHAPTER TWO
THREE JOURNEYS

Tears streamed down my face as the doors of the chopper slammed shut. As it began its ascent, I stood back wondering, *Will I ever see my little boy alive again?*[2]

2. *The Boy Who Came Back from Heaven* begins with a tragic automobile accident that occurred when Alex was six. He and his father were returning from church on a Sunday morning, when Kevin Malarkey, on his cell phone and reportedly distracted by Alex talking to him from the backseat, pulled directly into the path of an oncoming car.

The impact threw Kevin Malarkey from the Honda Civic. His son, still strapped into his seatbelt, sustained a severe spinal injury and was taken by MedFlight helicopter to Columbus Children's Hospital, where he would remain in a coma for two months.

CHAPTER THREE
72 HOURS

At last a medical assistant led Beth and me to a small conference room. The doctor wanted to speak with us privately.[3]

3. Malarkey's book sold 112,386 copies in its first year and three years later won a platinum award from the Evangelical Christian Publishers Association for having surpassed 1 million in sales. In addition, Tyndale House released an audio version, a DVD documentary based on the book, and sold the movie rights.

   I quote just the first two sentences of each of the ten chapters because the book remains under copyright.

   Beth was Malarkey's wife at the time of the accident, and the mother of Alex and three younger children. When the doctor spoke with Kevin and Beth privately, he showed them an x-ray of Alex's spinal injury and let them know that, if Alex were to survive, he would be paralyzed and likely unable to breathe on his own.

CHAPTER FOUR
AN ARMY GATHERS

Three days after the accident, I woke up and made my way to the shower. I had slept fitfully the night before.[4]

4. Alex spent a total of three months in Children's Hospital before returning home. The "army" referenced in the title of chapter 4 includes friends, family, and countless parishioners from the church the Malarkey family had been attending. These generous community members brought food and formed prayer groups at Alex's bedside. Good Samaritans also stepped in to pay some of the family's household bills and to complete structural repairs to the family home after a tree fell onto the roof during an ice storm.

CHAPTER FIVE
MIRACLES, MESSES, AND MORE MIRACLES

The sense of God's presence was becoming more palpable than I had ever known. Miracles were happening to Alex—though we did not yet know it.[5]

5. The not-as-yet-known miracle Malarkey refers to here is that Alex went to Heaven. And, as the title of the book promises, he came back.

Each chapter of *The Boy Who Came Back from Heaven* ends with a small section titled "From Alex," in which the boy describes the violent automobile crash from his perspective. Alex sees the oncoming car just before impact; he hears glass breaking, witnesses his father flying from the car, and imagines that his father is going to die. Moreover, as he hovers above the scene, Alex witnesses five angels supporting his father's body. "The angels were big and muscular, like wrestlers, and they had wings on their backs from their waists to their shoulders."

He sees the devil at the crash site as well, and the devil tells Alex that *he* is responsible for his father's death. Alex believes what Satan tells him, because he "had asked Daddy a question and he turned to answer my question right before the car hit us."

Moments later Alex is transported through a long white tunnel filled with "really bad music played on instruments with really long strings." And then the boy sees God, who has a human body "but it was a lot bigger."

Nowhere in the book is it explained when Alex's sections were written (presumably, of course, once Alex was out of his coma and able to communicate).

Some of the facts that we learn about Heaven include: (1) There is a tall gate separating inner Heaven from outer Heaven (the waiting room for new arrivals); (2) The gate has scales "like a fish"; (3) "There is a hole in outer Heaven. That hole goes to Hell."

We are told, though, that God asked Alex to not share too many more details.

CHAPTER SIX
WE MEET ANOTHER WORLD

As December approached, so many incredible things had happened since the accident that we sensed that, other than Alex's complete recovery, the biggest events were behind us. There had already been more than enough cause for praise.[6]

6. Roughly 5 percent of dying patients will describe having near-death experiences (or NDE), and these accounts often share similar details: a sense of floating, viewing the scene (a car accident, as in the case of Alex, a hospital emergency room, or a surgical table) from above, spending time in a beautiful, soothing locale (which many will identify as Heaven), and meeting welcoming beings, often dressed in white (and often described as angels). In most cases, the individual having the near-death experience reports feelings of joy, of transcendence, sometimes a spiritual awakening.

To the deeply religious, the explanation for these accounts, and their similarities, is obvious. Heaven, angels, and God all really do exist, and a fortunate few get to witness this and come back to tell the tale.

Scientists, not surprisingly, search for alternate explanations, examining the physiology, phenomenology, and aftereffects of near-death experience accounts. Various theories on what causes the NDE phenomena include oxygen deprivation, the effects of anesthesia, or neurochemical releases associated with extreme bodily trauma, but no consensus exists. Another intriguing theory posits that human consciousness is more complex than most of us realize, and NDE survivors who report "heavenly" visits have momentarily connected with levels of consciousness that exist for all of us, but that most of us never access.

CHAPTER SEVEN
HOMECOMINGS

It had been several months since Columbus Children's had become our home away from home. The ministry of God's people had kept our lives from completely unraveling, and we were deeply grateful.[7]

7. Though Kevin Malarkey's book offers an optimistic tone on almost every page, buoyed by God's grace and the helpfulness of the extended community of supporters, Malarkey mentions more than once the stress on his marriage brought about by the accident and its aftermath. "Most couples have the luxury of working out the kinks of their relationship in privacy," he writes in chapter 7, "but we were living our lives in the waiting room of Children's Hospital and in the midst of a home that had become Grand Central." He and Beth would often lose their tempers, he tells us, in front of strangers, their children, and the nurses and caretakers who visited them on a daily basis once Alex was released.

What Malarkey describes is certainly understandable, given the stresses posed by Alex's grave health challenges and the family's mounting medical bills. Malarkey, however, may not have been telling the full story. Though he paints an overall picture of two parents working as a team, sharing great optimism for Alex's full recovery, subsequent press accounts suggest the marriage had begun unraveling long before the book's publication and that care of Alex was not shared equally.

CHAPTER EIGHT
WAR AND PEACE

Time is a quiet miracle worker, healing, bestowing wisdom, and providing perspective. Time was doing its work, making routine that which was once traumatic.[8]

8. Dante's Eighth Circle, like the one before, is a crowded, miserable pit of despair, filled this time around with Panderers, Seducers, Flatterers, Simoniacs, Sorcerers, Hypocrites, Thieves, Evil Counselors, and Sowers of Discord. While Dante the character reacts with alarm and terror, Dante the poet is at his ghoulish best in this realm, offering some of the most vivid of his Hellish punishments.

For instance, Simonists, those church officials who sold ecclesiastical offices or indulgences, are embedded for eternity headfirst into slabs of rock, only their feet sticking up into the air. "From the calf up, inside. They twitched and shook // Because the soles of both feet were aflame—"

Farther along, false prophets have their heads twisted backward, "some cruel torsion / Forced face toward kidneys."

The bottom of the Eight Circle is reserved for the worst among them: Falsifiers, biting at one another, "the way a pig does loosed from the pen."

Dante spared no mercy.

The Eighth Circle, it may be worth noting, contains one of the more peculiar lines in all of Dante's decidedly peculiar *Inferno*. Dante and Virgil are in search of a way to cross the Sixth Bolgia (or ditch), but the bridge is damaged, so a team of scouts is sent to see if a bridge farther along the way is in working order. The signal for the exploratory team of sinners to march is a fart, or as Dante puts it, "And the leader made a trumpet of his ass."

Perhaps cranky old Alighieri had a sense of humor after all.

CHAPTER NINE
ENDINGS AND BEGINNINGS

The boy who came back from heaven was the son we knew, but something more. He had been "away from [his] earthly bod[y] . . . [and] at home with the Lord" (2 Corinthians 5:8), and the experience had changed him forever.[9]

---

9. Despite its considerable success, *The Boy Who Came Back from Heaven* was pulled from the shelves in 2015 after Alex Malarkey and his mother called into question both the truth of the book and Kevin Malarkey's right to publish it under Alex's name.

Among the claims, contained in a letter from Beth Malarkey to the publisher, Tyndale House, was that the car accident that paralyzed Alex for life was "caused by the negligence of his father, Kevin Malarkey." While Kevin, in the book, suggests that he was distracted by Alex calling out from the back seat, claiming he was hungry, Beth asserts that Alex "did not ask Kevin for food but was trying to warn Kevin of the car that he was able to see coming. Kevin is easily distracted."

In 2018 a lawsuit was filed in Alex's name, claiming that Kevin Malarkey had "concocted" the entire story, and that Alex had not received a penny of the book's substantial earnings. In fact, the lawsuit states, Alex and his mother (separated from Kevin) were living on Social Security payments and "on the verge of being homeless."

"Given the nature of the Book that Tyndale House published about Alex," the lawsuit states, "claiming that Alex had communicated with and interacted with God the Father, Jesus, angels, and the devil, any reasonable person would have realized that it was highly unlikely that the content of the Book was true."

The lawsuit continues to wind its way through the courts.

CHAPTER TEN
THE ROAD AHEAD

After all our confident assertions about Alex's full recovery, wouldn't it be great to end the book with a story about Alex waking up one morning miraculously healed, leaping out of bed, and racing to the front lawn to play football with Aaron or climb trees with Gracie? But reality is more complex—more beautiful than that.[10]

---

10. It would be great if Alex had woken up one morning miraculously healed, leapt out of bed, and raced to the front lawn to play football or climb trees. Sadly, though, no apparent miracles have occurred, and Alex still lives every day with the extreme damage to his spine.

Alex, it turns out, didn't go to Heaven. And as I may have mentioned before, Dante didn't really go to Hell.

Kevin Malarkey, on the other hand, maybe would, if Hell existed, because the response from his wife and son suggests the "Christian therapist" is also a false prophet, like those Dante condemned to unspeakable torture in his Eighth Circle.

What is it that makes people so willingly gullible, so eager to embrace a book that, even if you do believe in Heaven, rings false in so many moments? Alex, we are told, at the supposed moment of his death, was transported through a white tunnel filled with "really bad music played on instruments with really long strings." Does that somehow seem credible?

Religious charlatans appear throughout history, too numerous to catalog, some fleeting, some still revered by certain sects, cults, and organized religions. You'd think we'd be on to them by now.

Heaven is a fairly easy sell, I suppose. It is understandably comforting to those who suffer on Earth to think there will be an eventual reward, and one not only unbelievably sweet but infinite. Heaven, in fact, is such an appealing fairy tale that millions of people purchased a barely credible book by a guy whose last name happened to be Malarkey.

Look it up. The name itself should have been a giveaway.

But if Heaven seems a seductive fantasy, Hell still greatly confounds me.

I understand, of course, how the threat of ultimate punishment might have been helpful as a way to make regular folks behave back in those early times when the myth began, and I acknowledge the likely contribution the nightmare mythology provided toward moving the human race from disorganized, predatory packs toward a larger, civilized society. But it is 2020 as I write this, and we are a fairly sophisticated batch of human critters, so why do we still hang onto to the gruesome metaphor?

We've learned volumes about the various layers of the Earth's crust. No one has found a hole full of sinners.

We have identified and eliminated countless "portals" to hell. Turns out they are just caves.

It has been thousands upon thousands of years since the Old Testament stories were first shared, and no credible sightings of Satan have occurred lately.

The Buddhists likely have it right: Hell is of our own making. Act wickedly and karma follows.

Eventually.

The rest, it seems, is just ass trumpets and malarkey.

10

CANTOS
XXXI – XXXIV

CANTOS XXXI–XXXIV: BEYOND GOODE AND EVIL

ABANDON ALL

HOPE

Beyond Goode and Evil

It is not jokingly that one begins
To describe the bottom of the universe—
Not a task suited for a tongue that whines
~ Dante, *Inferno*, Canto XXXII

Be honest with me.

Have I been joking a bit too much in my attempts to describe the bottom of Dante's universe?

Perhaps.

Have I been whining?

Perhaps that too.

There are those reading these words who, undoubtedly, do not feel personally touched by the scourge of Dante, by the ashen pall of Augustine, by the depressive guilt brought on by religious malarkey, or by the corrosive juices simmering in the false stew of original sin.

I'm glad for that, actually. Better if none of us had borne the weight.

But we did, some of us. Many of us. Even those who were not aware of it, not keenly focused on how the Christian Bible and organized Christian religions have so thoroughly shaped the Western world and our experience of it.

We still swear on the Bible, after all, in court, or when assuming public office; even at the federal level, despite the supposed separation of church and state.

We imprison folks without hope of parole because we are convinced their inclination to break with "God's law" puts them beyond rehabilitation.

We still find Bibles tucked away in hotel rooms.

We feast visually on exquisite portraits of the baby Jesus and cringe at the gruesome torture of saints any time we walk through a good-sized art museum.

We say "Christ, Almighty!" almost reflexively, without considering what we have just uttered.

Christmas, of course, is everywhere. Just try to ignore it.

And our popular culture's current obsession with the Apocalypse and the "end of times" is a not-so-subtle echo of the Book of Revelation, perhaps?

You don't need to have endured twelve years of Catholic School, as I did, to be touched by the dark angel.

But in all my grumbling about old Dante and his nasty Florentine revenge fantasies, about the sin-ification of typical human urges, about hypocrisy, illogic, and pickles in the swill, there remains an open question.

A hole in my argument.

If Hell does not exist, if sin is just a man-made construct, what the Hell do we do with the existence of evil?

Because evil *is* out there.

I've seen it.

The Gates of Hell opened for me to witness, briefly, in 1985, in Philadelphia, when Mayor Wilson Goode and Police Commissioner Gregore Sambor authorized the dropping of military-grade explosives on a row house containing roughly thirteen people, including six children.

The story of how it came to that point is convoluted, contested, and tragic.

It goes like this:

A man named Vincent Leaphart went off to serve in the U.S. Army during the Korean War and during that time became disillusioned with his country, primarily with the racial and class divisions he saw both in the military and back at home. Once stateside, he became an activist and socialist, joining a community group that pooled money to buy houses in Philadelphia's impoverished Powelton neighborhood, just to the north of the University of Pennsylvania's idyllic, tree-lined urban campus.

Leaphart's ideas on race and class, along with a concern for animal rights, led him eventually to form what he called the American Christian Movement for Life. Group members picketed the Philadelphia Zoo, demonstrated outside a pet store, and notably, the *Philadelphia Inquirer* reports, once "handcuffed talk-show host Mike Douglas in his studio to retaliate for an episode in which an errant chimpanzee had been handcuffed and shot with a tranquilizer dart after running amok during a taping."

Over the next decade, as Leaphart's radicalism grew, he changed his name to John Africa, and his movement, now known as MOVE, attracted dozens of followers dedicated to a philosophy espousing a return to a hunter-gatherer society and a rejection of technology. In practice, this led to scavenging, the consumption of mostly raw foods, and communal living.

The collective house shared by many MOVE members began almost immediately to draw complaints from neighbors, regarding the number of dogs being kept on the property, the proliferation of rats and cockroaches, and the group's frequent use of a bullhorn to share John Africa's teachings with anyone passing by.

MOVE members were also known at times to stand outside the Powelton house brandishing weapons.

In August 1978, Philadelphia police officers were sent to the MOVE house to serve a court order to vacate. The resulting confrontation left one police officer dead and nine MOVE members jailed for life.

Three years later, what remained of the MOVE collective relocated to a mainly middle class, predominantly black West Philadelphia neighborhood known as Cobbs Creek, but it was not long before the new neighbors once again voiced complaints. The MOVE house, one of dozens of row houses crowded onto the 6200 block of Osage Avenue, was being fortified, windows were boarded shut, and eventually a wooden structure described as a "bunker" appeared on the roof. Garbage accumulated around the perimeter, various children living in the house were said to be kept out of school, and the group renewed their practice of using a loudspeaker to broadcast John Africa's message, which now included the demand that the nine jailed MOVE members be released from prison.

My wife, Renita, and I lived roughly two miles away, in a home owned by my wife's sister and her husband; we occupied the third floor, they lived on the first and second floors, along with our nephew Viktor. I was in my midtwenties, bouncing back then from job to job, in search of a viable career path.

Occasionally I would see MOVE members, distinctive in their dread-locks and quasi-military dress, proselytizing at Clark Park, where I played pick-up volleyball on Sunday afternoons. But I didn't know much about MOVE other than an occasional article in the newspaper. They seemed, to put it mildly, eccentric.

Viktor played high school tennis, and his matches were regularly held at Cobbs Creek Recreation Center, a few blocks away from Sixty-Second and Osage, so he had more direct experience. Even as he hit around tennis balls on a warm afternoon, he could hear a relentless stream of hate and profanities coming from the loudspeaker on the top of the MOVE compound's roof. It went on day and night.

It was Viktor who, around dinnertime on Monday, May 13, 1985, knocked on our apartment door and asked if he could go up to the roof. Our third-floor apartment had a stairwell that led to an unfinished attic space, and through the attic there was roof access up a rickety wooden ladder, leading to a panoramic view spanning most of West Philadelphia.

Earlier that day, Mayor Goode sent police to execute warrants on the MOVE members occupying the Osage house. Given the violence experienced during the 1978 Powelton confrontation, nearly five hundred police officers were dispatched this time around. Water and electricity were shut off throughout the neighborhood. Residents were evacuated, told to grab a few belongings because they'd likely have to be away overnight.

Commissioner Sambor used a police bullhorn to announce, "Attention, MOVE! This is America! You have to abide by the laws of the United States!" When group members refused to surrender, police lobbed tear gas and aimed high pressure water hoses at the house. Some of the adults inside fired back with semi-automatic weapons, and the situation disintegrated quickly.

Late in the afternoon, in a decision still under contentious debate, officials decided to drop two containers of C-4 explosives—police called them "entry devices," while many would later refer to them as bombs—from a helicopter, hoping to end the firing of automatic weapons by targeting the bunker-like construction on the roof.

It didn't turn out well, for anyone.

The C-4 explosives ignited cans of gasoline near the bunker, fire spread quickly from the MOVE house to adjoining row houses, firefighters were kept at a distance due to continuing threats of gunfire, the fire spread some more, and by the end of that evening, sixty-one houses had been destroyed.

Inside the compound, six adults and five children were dead. One woman, Ramona Africa, and one child, Birdie Africa, had escaped the flames, though Birdie was badly burned.

It was a comfortably warm May evening on the rooftop where Viktor, Renita, and I watched the circling helicopters, and the smoke, and the increasingly orange glow of the flames from our rooftop. But we knew, because we took turns slipping downstairs for updates, that what we were witnessing was horrible.

The siege, the bombing, and the spreading fire were carried live on local Philadelphia television. It is a cliché to say "we couldn't believe our eyes," but in this case it was entirely true, for us, and for many Philadelphians sitting in their living rooms, watching their own televisions, wondering how it all could have gone to Hell so fast.

Mayor Goode's reputation never fully recovered, and neither did the Osage neighborhood. The sixty-one destroyed homes were rebuilt, but poor construction practices resulted in numerous structural defects, including leaking roofs and sagging floors. The contractors were eventually sent to jail.

A year after the fire, my wife and I participated in the nationwide charity event known as Hands Across America. Approximately 6.5 million people attempted to form a human chain from coast to coast by holding hands. (The chain part was unsuccessful, though the event raised millions.) Renita and I were part of the chain that circled Philadelphia City Hall, and just six or so spots up the row from us I spotted Mayor Goode.
I waved.
He smiled.
He didn't look evil.
He looked tired.

To be entirely clear, when I say that I've seen evil firsthand, I'm not sure if I mean Mayor Goode and whatever testosterone-riddled police officials convinced him that dropping military grade c-4 explosives by helicopter might be a sensible way to take down the MOVE bunker, or if I mean the angry MOVE members I crossed paths with at Clark Park, the disgruntled radicals who cruelly terrorized residents on and near Osage Avenue, and who, ultimately, are responsible for putting the six children's lives at risk.
At the time, most folks were happy to blame Goode. Many still do.
Others said of the MOVE dead, "They got what they deserved."
We could easily, instead, blame poverty. Housing inequality. Racism. Guns.
Maybe Vincent Leaphart.
We could blame hopelessness.
Dante, after all, warned us:
Abandon hope, all ye who enter here.

I don't, however, blame Satan.

No one reported seeing him at the scene that evening. The smoke and flames from the Osage fire did not portentously swirl about *Fantasia*-like to reveal his cartoon face.

These were man-made circumstances, man-made decisions, and if Hell opened up in May 1985, mortal men were pushing at the gates, and the Hell that opened was the Hell we carry inside of us.

An ugly, perilous hole.

EPILOGUE

EPILOGUE: MY PARADISO

SELF

LOATHING

My Paradiso (with Basil and Tomato Cream)

Through a round aperture I saw appear

Some of the beautiful things that Heaven bears,
Where we came forth, and once more saw the stars.
~ Dante, *Inferno*, Canto XXXIV

The *Inferno* is just the first of three books comprising the *Commedia*, though it is by far the most widely read and clearly the most recognized.

Dante ends the opening installment of his trilogy with good old Butch and Sundance[1] grabbing frozen tufts of greasy hair to climb Lucifer's muscled legs, the ladder by which they escape Hades and return to "the shining world," where they once again can see the twinkling stars.

But the sad truth is this: there is no rest for our intrepid chroniclers of the wild and wicked beyond.

Soon enough, Dante has set forth for *Purgatorio*, eager to reconnoiter a big rock candy mountain where sins are purged and sinners (only those lucky ones who have sidestepped Hell on some technicality) are somehow washed clean enough that they can ascend to the long-anticipated, "Sitting-at-the-Big-Feet-of-Our-Lord" place called Heaven.

Among the first sinners Dante encounters in the second installment of his trilogy are several hapless souls stumbling under the crushing weight of the mammoth boulders they bear on their backs. The sinners beat at their breasts, forever lamenting the painful burdens they carry.

---

1. Yes, I had considered Gilligan and the Skipper here. Also, maybe, Thelma and Louise, but they don't survive.

Well, exactly!

Dante's boulder-crushed sinners are the perfect metaphor for the massive emotional backpacks of needless guilt that have been strapped onto our tender psyches by organized religion and the pretzel-logic of medieval theology.

Gee! It is almost as if Dante and I agree.

And then comes *Paradiso*, the least-read portion of Dante's three-part poem, unpopular perhaps because the plot has become so utterly predictable.

One more time, still seeking respite from the "tangled, and rough / And savage" woods of middle age,[2] Dan and Virge climb through layers of the afterworld, encountering long-dead Biblical celebrities and yet a few more of Dante's old pals from Florence (including Beatrice, his first love, now in a starring role).

The poet bases his fictional heaven on the celestial sphere theory, championed long before by Aristotle, Ptolemy, and Copernicus, and by now, well-debunked.[3]

In other words, Dante's Heavenly fantasy is based entirely on false science, which is no big surprise, since Dante's visions have all along been clever but baseless. Just as much of what is being taught by organized religions is ultimately so much hooey.

I ask again:

Why can't we just dispense with this superstition? Black cats don't bring bad luck and stepping on a crack is highly unlikely to break anyone's back, much less your mother's.

It isn't helping.

---

2. Miraculously, he never mentions his aching knees or swollen prostate.
3. The celestial sphere theory posits that the Earth is at the center of everything. Putting our planet, and its human inhabitants, smack dab in the middle of the universe was a narcissistic lynchpin of early theology. Why? Because, if we were not so prominently placed, then why would God be so focused on our every weakness or bad decision?

The origin of life, the shape and purpose of the universe, the inexplicable reasons behind our magical and fortuitous existence, cannot be grasped by our inadequate human intelligence, at least not yet. Nor can the answers to all these puzzles be put into words, no matter how poetic these words may be, whether presented in *terza rima* or as a lopsided limerick.[4]

And surely, this grand mystery of creation and life, whatever the explanation, is not something that can be neatly packaged into a strict set of rules and punishments, hung on the door of a church, and used to order the actions of mankind for century upon century.

Religion is an attempt to explain what we cannot know, and the attempt inevitably fails.

Dante's Hell makes no sense. In his *Inferno*, the damned are placed in specific horrific locales based on their sin against God, but who do we know that is guilty of only one type of sin? We weak-willed humans tend to feast at the smorgasbord—a little lust, a bit of gluttony, maybe some anger, a dash of heresy here and there.[5]

It's all metaphor, of course, so don't take it seriously.

But Sister Mary Mark did.

And we little babies, sitting in our desks at the back of religion class at St. Andrew's Catholic School, fingering the nickels in our pockets and wondering whether it was better to give them over to the poor neglected pagan babies or to have a pint-sized carton of cold chocolate milk with our lunches that day, were encouraged to take it as God's word, despite the countless logical contradictions.

---

4. There once was a father from Heaven
   Not sure, but let's call him Kevin
   "Behave," he insisted
   But our free will resisted
   And thus we're all going to . . . um . . . Hell.
5. Not to mention, picking up grapes that have fallen in our vineyard. Being born on a Sunday. Trimming our beards.

I am truly grateful that I was not required to scurry through the underworld and climb up Lucifer's matted leg hairs out into the open air in order to see the stars again. My transformation was gradual, starting in first grade and growing in intensity over time, but, all in all, less traumatic than the fictional Dante's journey.

But it weren't perfect.

I've found myself in my own dark woods, the right way lost, with depressing regularity, off and on, here and there, for most of my life. Along the way my shadowy moods, my seething frustrations, my anger hurt the people I love the most.

My wife. My daughter. Myself.

Depression and the mood swings that sometimes come with depression are both hard to describe, because they defy logic. I could become furious over how knives were stored in the silverware drawer. I could go dark for days, brooding, off in my own corner, because I felt underappreciated. *Don't they see how hard I work?*

When overcoming my dark moods seemed too difficult, I would succumb, cowardly and afraid, allowing my depressive pall to become the new normal, which all too easily spread to those around me.

Mistake after mistake after mistake, now just history.

I'm not naïve enough to believe that all would have been well in my life if the early Christian theologians hadn't codified Hell, or if St. Augustine hadn't marked us with original sin, or if Dante hadn't pounded all of it into our culture like some crucifixion nail.

But did it help?

Nah.

There is much I regret, and much I cannot undo. That burden is genuine.

Yet here is the good part:

Along the way, each time that ugly snake of despair circled around and tried to take another bite out of me, I was kept alive by humor and by incredulity.

And thank God for humor and incredulity, because I deserve to be happy.

We all deserve to be happy.

"Anything that will keep you warm in the winter will keep you cool in the summer," Walter promised me at the Darke County Steam Threshers flea market.

I am still unsure whether to laugh or throw my arms up in disbelief.

Humor or incredulity?

I choose both.

If Walter was a divine messenger of some sort, here is what he was probably trying to tell me:

Anything that keeps you alive in the darker times will, at the very least, afford you a modicum of time to find your way out, a chance to locate your own paradise, even a small patch of it, maybe just a cool breeze on a sweltering summer day.

Or maybe he was just having me on.

What is Paradise, after all?

Maybe a plate of warm tagliolini with basil and tomato cream in a cozy restaurant near the Ponte Vecchio in Dante's beloved Florence. But not back then, of course: now, in the age of electricity and reliable air conditioning. Beyond the bitter theological battles.

Maybe the waitress in this cozy restaurant is named Nora, and maybe she reminds me of my second-grade crush. I crack a dumb joke and she laughs. Maybe there is wine, and a palate-pleasing arugula and goat cheese salad.

And after an Amaro Lucano, when I finally saunter from Ristorante dei Sottaceti into the evening dusk, I don't hate myself for overeating, I don't condemn myself for the little square of tiramisu, or for buying too many touristy postcards. I am just fine being me, because I am just fine.

And maybe I stroll to the Piazza del Duomo, stand near the imposing bronze doors of the Baptistery de San Giovanni, where young Dante was baptized, before he grew so spiteful and angry. Maybe I see a man who looks vaguely like my father. He is smiling, sitting cross-legged on the marble steps, holding hands with his son.

Maybe Sister Mary Mark crosses my path just then and says, "You know, I'm sorry. In retrospect, I probably shouldn't have scared you all so much. I maybe should have listened now and then."

And maybe I forgive her.

And maybe I remember Steamboat Willie and Periwinkle. Those pagan babies surreptitiously baptized in the dark of night.

And maybe that gives me reason to look up at the twinkling stars.

And then, perhaps, the most amazing thing happens.

Maybe I don't feel that deep emptiness.

Maybe there is no Hole.

Maybe I forgive myself.

ACKNOWLEDGMENTS

All passages quoted from *Dante's Inferno* are taken from *The Inferno of Dante: A New Verse Translation*, trans. Robert Pinsky (New York: Farrar, Straus and Giroux, 1994).

I would like to thank the many individuals who helped me with research, listened to my odd and occasionally misguided musings on religion, steered me toward useful resources, and generously tolerated me while I scribbled away at this book.

Specific gratitude to Mary Kate Hurley, Eric and Kristin LeMay, Rodger Kamenetz, Viktor Votsch, Samuel Autman, Joe Heithaus, Tommy Shea and Suzanne Strempek Shea, David Lynn and the entire *Kenyon Review* Writers Workshop crowd.

Thank you as well to Dr. J. David Field, Dianne L. Hardin, and DePauw University for affording me extra writing hours during my semester as the 2018–19 Mary Rogers Field and Marion Field-McKenna Distinguished University Professor for Creative Writing.

And to Brandon, Walter, and all the other kind folks I met along the way.

INDEX

How to Survive Death and
Other Inconveniences
by Sue William Silverman

The Pat Boone Fan Club: My Life
as a White Anglo-Saxon Jew
by Sue William Silverman

Scraping By in the Big Eighties
by Natalia Rachel Singer

Sky Songs: Meditations on
Loving a Broken World
by Jennifer Sinor

In the Shadow of Memory
by Floyd Skloot

Secret Frequencies: A New
York Education
by John Skoyles

The Days Are Gods
by Liz Stephens

Phantom Limb
by Janet Sternburg

When We Were Ghouls: A
Memoir of Ghost Stories
by Amy E. Wallen

Yellowstone Autumn: A Season of
Discovery in a Wondrous Land
by W. D. Wetherell

This Fish Is Fowl: Essays of Being
by Xu Xi

To order or obtain more information on these or other
University of Nebraska Press titles, visit nebraskapress.unl.edu.

9 781496 224606